J. K. Rowling's
Harry Potter Novels
A Reader's Guide

(This book has not been authorized by J. K. Rowling or Warner Bros.)

CONTINUUM CONTEMPORARIES
Also available in this series

Pat Barker's *Regeneration*, by Karin Westman
Kazuo Ishiguro's *The Remains of the Day*, by Adam Parkes
Carol Shields's *The Stone Diaries*, by Abby Werlock
Jane Smiley's *A Thousand Acres*, by Susan Farrell
Louis De Bernieres's *Captain Corelli's Mandolin*, by Con Coroneos
Irvine Welsh's *Trainspotting*, by Robert Morace
Barbara Kingsolver's *The Poisonwood Bible*, by Linda Wagner-Martin
Donna Tartt's *The Secret History*, by Tracy Hargreaves
Toni Morrison's *Paradise*, by Kelly Reames

Forthcoming in this series

Annie Proulx's *The Shipping News*, by Aliki Varvogli
Kate Atkinson's *Behind the Scenes at the Museum*, by Emma Parker
Haruki Murakami's *The Wind-up Bird Chronicle*, by Matthew Strecher
Jonathan Coe's *What a Carve Up!*, by Pamela Thurschwell
Don DeLillo's *Underworld*, by John Duvall
Graham Swift's *Last Orders*, by Pamela Cooper
Michael Ondaatje's *The English Patient*, by John Bolland
Ian Rankin's *Black and Blue*, by Gill Plain
Bret Easton Ellis's *American Psycho*, by Julian Murphet
Cormac McCarthy's *All the Pretty Horses*, by Stephen Tatum
Iain Banks's *Complicity*, by Cairns Craig
A. S. Byatt's *Possession*, by Catherine Burgass
David Guterson's *Snow Falling on Cedars*, by Jennifer Haytock
Helen Fielding's *Bridget Jones's Diary*, by Imelda Whelehan
Sebastian Faulks's *Birdsong*, by Pat Wheeler
Hanif Kureishi's *The Buddha of Suburbia*, by Nahem Yousaf
Nick Hornby's *High Fidelity*, by Joanne Knowles
Zadie Smith's *White Teeth*, by Claire Squires
Arundhati Roy's *The God of Small Things*, by Julie Mullaney
Alan Warner's *Morvern Callar*, by Sophy Dale
Vikram Seth's *A Suitable Boy*, by Angela Atkins
Margaret Atwood's *Alias Grace*, by Gina Wisker

· **J. K. ROWLING'S**

Harry Potter Novels

A READER'S GUIDE

PHILIP NEL

CONTINUUM | NEW YORK | LONDON

2001

The Continuum International Publishing Group, Inc.
370 Lexington Avenue, New York, NY 10017

The Continuum International Publishing Group Ltd.
The Tower Building, 11 York Road, London SE1 7NX

www.continuumbooks.com

Printed in the United States of America

Library of Congress Cataloging-in-Publication Data

Nel, Philip, 1969–
  J. K. Rowling's Harry Potter novels/Philip Nel.
    p. cm.—(Continuum contemporaries)
  Includes bibliographical references.
  ISBN 0-8264-5232-9 (pbk.: alk. paper)
  1. Rowling, J. K.—Characters—Harry Potter. 2. Potter, Harry (fictitious
character) 3. Children's stories, English—History and criticism.
4. Fantasy fiction, English—History and criticism. 5. Wizards in literature. 6. Magic in literature. I. Title. II. Series.

PR6068.O93 Z79 2001
823'.914—dc21   2001032579

Contents

Acknowledgments

After acknowledging the fine work of the Jack Hardman Clipping Service, I thank Naomi Wood and Gloria Hardman for offering helpful suggestions on improving the manuscript. Thanks, too, to Mark Osteen for keeping his ear to the ground and to Pierre Nel for taking an interest in his son's curious pursuits. Last but definitely most, extra slices of chocolate-covered thanks to Karin Westman for her support, intelligence, and love.

The Novelist

When, in the first chapter of the first Harry Potter novel, Professor Minerva McGonagall predicts that the infant Harry Potter "will be famous—a legend—[. . .] there will be books written about Harry—every child will know his name" (*Philosopher's Stone* 15), she proves worthy of her namesake. Harry became famous when he was but a year old, and J. K. Rowling has attained her character's degree of fame in her early thirties—rather late in life compared with Harry, but remarkably quick when compared with anyone else. On July 31, 1965 (exactly 25 years before Harry's birth, in the time frame of the novels), in Gloucestershire, Joanne Kathleen Rowling[1] was born to Peter and Anne Rowling at Chipping Sodbury General Hospital, a place "appropriate for someone who collects funny names," Rowling later observed (Rowling, "Not Especially"). Her father, a chartered engineer for Rolls-Royce, and her mother, a lab technician of French and Scottish descent, had met a few years earlier on a train heading from London's King's Cross station to Abroath, Scotland. Rowling describes her parents' meeting as "love at first sight" (Fraser, *Telling Tales* 4), and Peter proposed to Anne on another train, fueling their future daughter's love of trains. In about

1964, they married, and two years after Joanne's birth, a second daughter, Diana (nicknamed Di) was born.

Early Childhood

Both Anne and Peter Rowling loved reading, read to their children, and by the time she was six, Joanne began inventing stories which she told to her younger sister. In an autobiographical essay, Rowling says that one such story involved Di falling down a rabbit hole and being "fed strawberries by the rabbit family inside." However, the first narrative Rowling wrote down "was about a rabbit called Rabbit. He got the measles and was visited by his friends, including a giant bee called Miss Bee" ("Not Especially"). Upon finishing this story, the six-year-old Joanne thought, "Well now we can publish this." Looking back on it, Rowling explains, "I wanted the complete experience, even then" (Fraser 9). Ever since writing about Rabbit and Bee, Rowling wanted to be a writer, though she "rarely told anyone so," because she feared "they'd tell me I didn't have a hope" ("Not Especially").

Shortly after penning the "rabbit tale," the Rowlings moved from Yate to Winterbourne (both towns are near Bristol), living in a house four doors down from the Potters. Jo and Di became friends with the Potter children, Vikki and Ian. Ian was fond of playing tricks on his friends, including hiding slugs on picnic plates and persuading his sister and the Rowling girls to run through wet concrete (into which they promptly sank) (Cochrane). Given his proclivity for practical jokes, Ian sounds much more like Fred and George Weasley than Harry, and, according to Rowling, she chose his family name for her title character simply because she "always liked the name" Potter ("Not Especially"). However, Vikki suspects that Rowling may have named her hero "Potter" because she, her brother, and the Rowling sisters used to play at witches and wizards (Demetriou).

When Rowling was nine, her family left the Potters' neighbor-hood, moving north of the Severn River to settle in Tutshill, near Chepstow, in Wales. She disliked her new school, Tutshill Primary, a small, old-fashioned building near her house. Mrs. Morgan, her new teacher, influenced the character of Severus Snape, the severe Hogwarts professor who plays favorites and bullies Harry and his friends (Fraser 5–6). On her very first morning at Tutshill Primary, Morgan gave Joanne an arithmetic test on fractions, a subject that Rowling had not studied. After she failed the test, her teacher placed her in "the 'stupid' row": In Mrs. Morgan's class, "the brightest sat on her left, and everyone she thought was dim sat on the right." Rowling was placed "as far right as you could get without sitting in the playground." When, by the end of the year, she had been pro-moted to the second row from the left, her teacher forced Rowling to switch seats with her best friend. In "that one short walk across the room," Rowling recalls, "I became clever but unpopular" ("Not Especially").

Early Literary Influences

While enduring the injustices inflicted by her formal education, Rowling enjoyed reading and continued to write stories, including one about seven cursed diamonds (Transcript of J. K. Rowling's live interview, Feb. 3, 2000). Some of the books she read between the ages of eight and twelve include Paul Gallico's *Manxmouse* (1968), Elizabeth Goudge's *The Little White Horse* (1946), C. S. Lewis's *Narnia* series (1950–1956), as well as novels by E. Nesbit and Noel Streatfeild. Her "diamond story" suggests an interest in the mystery, the literary form that endows the *Harry Potter* novels with such a strong narrative drive. The tone employed by both Gallico's and Nes-bit's narrators is alternately playful and serious, likely influencing

Rowling's narrative voice. Gallico's Clutterbumph, which strives to take the form of whatever will frighten Manxmouse the most, behaves much as the Boggart does in the third Harry Potter book. Most significant, perhaps, is that in the books of Nesbit, Gallico, and Goudge, fantasy and the everyday co-exist: the characters do not need to travel to another land (say, Narnia) to experience the magical. Just as Rowling's witches and wizards share the same world with Muggles, in Nesbit's *The Five Children and It* (1902), a sand fairy lives nearby, and in the sequel, *The Phoenix and the Carpet* (1904), the new carpet is magic and contains a phoenix egg. In contrast, the Narnia books seem an antecedent more in their epic confrontation between good and evil, albeit with more explicitly Christian theology than in Rowling's series. Streatfeild's tales of young people learning a profession echo the emphasis on practice in the Hogwarts classrooms where Harry and his friends learn witchcraft. In her own early life, however, Rowling seems to have gained professional training more outside of school than in it: With the possible exception of one English teacher, Rowling's extracurricular reading, writing, and playing shaped her more than her lessons did.

By age eleven, Rowling was attending Wydean Comprehensive, where she had Miss Shepherd, an English teacher who strongly brings to mind Professor McGonagall at Hogwarts. Rowling, who remains in touch with Shepherd, remembers her as "no-nonsense" and "strict," but also as "very conscientious." A feminist and "passionate about teaching," Ms. Shepherd earned Rowling's respect and taught her a great deal about how to write, Rowling remembers (Fraser 6). Refusing to permit her students "to be the least bit sloppy," Shepherd showed them "exactly what gave writing structure and pace" (Fraser 6–7). Influenced by her own wide reading as well as by Shepherd, Rowling writes tightly structured sentences and carefully paces the plot, holding the reader's attention by withholding just the right amount of information. Consider the following description of the journey to Hogwarts: "The rain thickened as the train sped yet further north; the windows were now a solid shimmering grey, which gradually darkened until lanterns flickered into life all along the corridors and over the luggage racks. The train rattled, the rain hammered, the wind roared, but still, Professor Lupin slept" (*Prisoner of Azkaban* 64). The rain "thickened" instead of just increased; the windows do not merely fog over but are "a solid shimmering grey." Keen attention to the sounds of words and the images they create allows Rowling to build suspense efficiently. The parallelism of the second sentence bundles together "rattled," "hammered," and "roared," amplifying the sensations evoked by the first while increasing the reader's curiosity about Professor Lupin. One expects that Miss Shepherd's advice may have been a version of William Strunk and E. B. White's dictum to omit needless words. "Vigorous writing is concise," they advise. Succinct prose requires not short sentences without detail, but "that every word tell" (23). Rowling's writing shows that she has learned this lesson well.

School Days

Though she has been accused of being an apologist for boarding schools, Rowling never attended one, and in any case, the world beyond her formal education provided abundant fascination. Rowling's house was right next to a graveyard ("I still love graveyards—they are great source of names," she admits [Fraser 4]), and she describes Tutshill as "a town dominated by a castle on a cliff, which might explain a lot" (Fraser 3). Phyl Lewis, a sculptor who taught Rowling ceramics at Wydean, believes that her former pupil's imaginative landscape springs directly from growing up in Tutshill. "You couldn't live near the Forest of Dean and the Wye valley and not be inspired," she observes. "The place is steeped in history, tradition and superstition. There's a magic to it." In her *Sunday Times* article "Harry's home," Lynne Cochrane visited Church Cottage, the Tutshill house where Rowling's family lived, and spoke with Lewis and other residents, all of whom were quick to find parallels with Rowling's novels. Despite the nearby motorway, Tushill feels "remote" and secretive; just as Harry and company move between the boundaries of different worlds, Tutshill is on the border between England and Wales, nestled between the Wye and Severn rivers. While we cannot know the degree to which the countryside nurtured her imagination, it may bear noting that in this same valley, Wordsworth wrote "Lines Composed a Few Miles above Tintern Abbey" (1798), which recalls wanderings along "the deep rivers, [. . .] the lonely streams," "the tall rock,/The mountain, and the deep and gloomy wood." Rowling's recollections of herself and her sister spending "most" of their time "wandering unsupervised across the fields and along the river Wye" ("Not Especially") or "exploring amongst the boulders" (Fraser 4) may not prove that "the deep and gloomy wood" inspired the Forbidden Forest or other *Harry Potter* locations, but they do emphasize the impression that it left on Rowling's aesthetic sensibility.

When not exploring the countryside, Rowling attended school. At first, she feared Wydean might be as bad as Tutshill Primary. Rowling heard the same rumor about Wydean that Harry hears from Dudley about Stonewall High: "They stuff people's heads down the toilet first day" (*Philosopher's Stone* 28). Probably a tale intended to scare first-year students, this threat of lavatory mischief was never carried out (at least, not against her). More studious than athletic, Rowling describes herself at this time as "quiet, freckly, short-sighted and rubbish at sports." Yet, when the toughest girl in her year picked a fight with her, Rowling fought back, becoming briefly famous for standing up to the bully. Her response to this triumph reveals her acute sense of the emotional landscape of childhood: "I spent weeks afterwards peering nervously around corners in case she was waiting to ambush me" ("Not Especially"). Appropriately, Rowling identifies with E. Nesbit, adding that Nesbit's claim, "I remember exactly how I felt and thought at 11," has "struck a chord with me" (J. K. Rowling's Bookshelf). Just as Oswald in *The Story of the Treasure Seekers* (1899) shows that E. Nesbit remembers what it is like to be eleven, so Harry, Ron, and Hermione testify to Rowling's ability to convey authentically the fears and joys of growing up. Aside from her encounter with the bully, most of Rowling's battles took place in the "long serial stories" she told her circle of friends during lunch: "too swotty" to be heroes in real life, the group became heroes as characters in Rowling's fictional world ("Not Especially"). Her "oldest friend," Séan Harris, whom she would meet at Wydean, inspired Ron Weasley ("JK Rowling Chat"). Rowling says that she herself at age eleven was "never as clever or annoying" as Hermione Granger ("Stories from the Web") but was very like her in other respects: "on the surface a proper little smart ass, but underneath quite insecure" (Johnstone, "Happy ending").

Reading Austen

After Hermione dashes off to the library yet again, Harry asks, "why's she got to go to the library?" Ron replies, "Because that's what Hermione does [. . .]. When in doubt, go the library" (*Chamber of Secrets* 189). Like Hermione, Joanne at age twelve was a good student and an avid reader. It was during this period of her life that she became a fan of Jane Austen, whom Rowling frequently mentions as her favorite writer, naming *Emma* (1815) as her favorite novel. She cites approvingly Virginia Woolf's memorable description of Austen: "For a great writer, she was the most difficult to catch in the act of greatness."[3] "You're drawn into the story," Rowling says, "you know you've seen something great in action," but "you can't see the pyrotechnics; there's nothing flashy" ("J. K. Rowling's Bookshelf"). It's true that there's nothing flashy, but the greatness of both Austen and Rowling lies in the subtlety and dexterity with which they set their plots in motion. Their novels reward the careful reader and encourage rereading: apparently minor details frequently turn out to have much larger significance. Only upon rereading do we see the portent of Knightley warning Emma against matchmaking in the first chapter ("You are more likely to have done harm to yourself, than good to them, by your interference"), just as returning to *Philosopher's Stone* after *Prisoner of Azkaban* highlights the significance of the apparently insignificant Sirius Black, who is briefly mentioned in the first chapter of *Philosopher's Stone*. The scenes late in the novel during which Emma re-evaluates her perceptions—"Every moment had brought a fresh surprise" and "How to understand the deceptions she had been [. . .] living under!" she thinks—recur in one form or another at the end of every *Harry Potter* novel, but most notably during the stunning denouement of *Prisoner of Azkaban*, when Harry, Ron, and Hermione re-evaluate their misperceptions of Sirius Black, Remus Lupin, and even Scabbers. As Rowling herself says of *Emma*, "it is the most skillfully managed mystery I've ever read" ("Let me tell you a story").

Suggestive of Rowling's affection for Austen, there's something very eighteenth century (or at least very early nineteenth century) about the way that *Harry Potter's* characters communicate by mail, with everyone gathering around as they read their letters. Dudley's television set, computer, and PlayStation remind us that the novels do take place in the 1990s, and anyone paying careful attention will notice that the cake at Nearly Headless Nick's 500th deathday party fixes his date of death in 1492, indicating that *Harry Potter and the Chamber of Secrets* takes place during the 1992–1993 school year (102). These facts notwithstanding, Hogwarts and the wizarding world retain practices that seem charmingly antique in an age of e-mail and the Internet. This is not to suggest that letters being de-livered by "Owl post" or characters writing with quills render the Harry Potter novels "old-fashioned" or out of touch with contemporary Britain. Even more than Amy Heckerling's *Clueless* (1995), the revision of *Emma* which brought Austen's satirical spirit into 1990s California, Rowling's novels satirize social behaviors. Though Rowling, like Austen, does give characters names that connote their character traits (Knightley in *Emma* or the wicked Wickham in *Pride and Prejudice*), Rowling's sense of humor leans more toward caricature, and her names sound more Dickensian: Gilderoy Lockhart, the vain, fatuous writer; Rita Skeeter, the shrilly persistent reporter; and Ludo Bagman, the corrupt, exuberant ex-Quidditch star. However, as in the novels of Rowling's literary idol, even the least important characters have a full history, as evidenced by the consistency throughout the series: when a minor character turns out to be a major character, Rowling clearly has known it all along.

From Head Girl to University Graduate

If her ability to surprise readers resides in selectively revealing what she already knows, Rowling's own life has delivered a series of blows she could not have anticipated. In 1980, when Rowling was fifteen, her mother was diagnosed with multiple sclerosis, an event that left a deep impression and, at least in part, contributes to her characterization of Professor Remus Lupin. One of the series' most appealing characters, Lupin also suffers from an incurable condition, though his was inflicted by a childhood werewolf bite. People shun him despite his intelligence, kindness, and the fact that he can take a potion that renders him docile during his transformations into a werewolf. Perhaps hinting at her mother's experiences, Rowling has said that Lupin's "being a werewolf is really a metaphor for people's reactions to illness and disability" (Fraser 22). Alleviating some of the sadness of living with a dying parent, Séan Harris entered her life when she was in the Upper Sixth form, soon becoming her best friend. The "getaway driver and foulweather friend" to whom *Harry Potter and the Chamber of Secrets* (1998) is dedicated, Harris whisked her away in his turquoise Ford Anglia, relieving her from the pain of her mother's illness and the boredom of being a teenager growing up in the country. So, in *Chamber of Secrets*, "I couldn't just have any old car rescuing Harry and Ron Weasley to take them to Hogwarts—it *had* to be a turquoise Ford Anglia," Rowling says (Fraser 7). "Harry was rescued by that car, just as the car rescued me from my boredom" (8).

Bored or not, Rowling showed herself to be as bright as Hermione, receiving top marks in her classes and becoming Head Girl in her final year at Wydean. After taking her A-level exams in French, German, and English, she went to the University of Exeter, some 120 kilometers (75 miles) south of Tutshill. Partly following her parents' advice that languages would lead to a promising career as a bilingual secretary and partly out of a genuine interest in languages, Rowling studied French as well as Greek and Roman Studies. Perhaps anticipating a different future for herself, Rowling—as part of her degree—spent a year in Paris as a teaching assistant. Motivated more by love of words than by the prospect of secretarial employment, she began collecting odd names more avidly than she had before, with her course of study influencing the names she would give her characters. "Malfoy" and "Voldemort" are derived from the French "bad faith" and "flight of death," respectively. Likewise, Argus Filch's name reveals as much about his personality as it does about Rowling's background in the classics: Ovid's *Metamorphoses* tells of the hundred-eyed Argus, whom Juno ordered to watch Io. When coupled with "filch" (meaning to pilfer, especially something of small value), "Argus" captures the petty, vigilant Hogwarts caretaker, ever eager to punish students for the tiniest infraction.

Still timid about revealing her interest in becoming an author, Rowling graduated from Exeter intending to begin the career that she had been advised to pursue. After receiving her degree in 1986, she moved to a flat in Clapham, South London, and enrolled in a bilingual secretarial course. Though she admits being ill-suited to secretarial work, Rowling finds it "incredibly useful" that she learned to type, because she now types all her books (Fraser 18). Perhaps inspired by the radical spirit of Jessica Mitford's *Hons and Rebels,* a book that "changed [her] life" when she read it at age fourteen, Rowling also worked as a research assistant for Amnesty International, investigating human rights abuses in Francophone Africa (Carey; Fraser 19). During her lunch hours, Rowling continued to invent stories, but instead of telling them to her friends as she did at Wydean, she wrote them down. Though she was not yet working on the *Harry Potter* novels, one wonders whether Hermione's Society for the Promotion of Elfish Welfare (S.P.E.W.) parodies the earnestness of Rowling's political activism at this stage of her life. Within a couple of years of graduating from Exeter, Rowling worked as a secretary, typing her stories on the office computer "when no-one was looking" and, rather than taking notes during meetings, writing stories and character names in the margins of her notepads ("Not Especially"). When showing a journalist some of the scrap paper in her boxes full of notes, Rowling observed, "This is my employment history—it's the back of stuff I really should have been doing as work, and on the front you have bits of my writing" (Stahl). Rowling had not yet found her calling, but her calling had found her: during these first few post-varsity years, she wrote two (unpublished) adult novels.

Birth of Harry

In 1990, Rowling moved from London to Manchester with her boyfriend. After a weekend spent seeking a flat in Manchester, she sat in a train, traveling the more than 250 kilometers back to London. While staring out of the window and "thinking of nothing in particular," she recalls, "the idea for Harry just kind of fell into my head. It was the purest stroke of inspiration I've ever had. Harry arrived pretty much fully formed. I could see him, I could see his little round glasses and I could see his scar. He was a very real boy to me from the beginning" (Adler). As luck would have it, the train was delayed, and Rowling did not have a working pen. Instead of asking to borrow one, she sat and thought for four hours, character after character appearing in her mind: Nearly Headless Nick, Peeves the poltergeist, Hermione, Ron, and Harry (Loer; Solomon). Even as she first saw him, Rowling understood that Harry would not know he was a wizard but had unconsciously been able to make odd things happen all his life without quite knowing why. She knew that since birth his name had been down at a prestigious school of witchcraft and wizardry. She realized, too, that his adoptive parents had hidden this from him, hoping they would "be able to squash the magic out of him" (Adler). Returning to Manchester, Rowling continued to be obsessed with the boy wizard's story even as her own life turned in unexpected directions. After a row with her boyfriend, she went to the pub at the Bourneville Hotel in Didsbury, and invented Quidditch (Fraser 23; "Magic, Mystery, and Mayhem").

Six months after she first got the idea for Harry Potter, Rowling's mother died at the age of forty-five. Rowling later acknowledged that she had given Harry her own feelings of grief (Hattenstone). In *Harry Potter and the Philosopher's Stone*, Harry sees his parents in the Mirror of Erised and feels "a powerful kind of ache inside him, half joy, half terrible sadness" (153). Asked what she would see in the Mirror of Erised, Rowling answers, "I would probably see my mother, who died in 1990. So, the same as Harry" (Barnes and Noble). Rowling's and Harry's longings resurface in *Harry Potter and the Prisoner of Azkaban*, when Harry recalls his mistaken belief that he had seen his father the night before. Harry remarks, "It was stupid, thinking it was him." Dumbledore replies, "Do you think the dead we have loved ever truly leave us? [. . .] Your father is alive in you, Harry, and shows himself most plainly when you have need of him" (312). Whether hearing his mother's final screams when Dementors torment him or encountering his parents' ghostly visages near the end of *Harry Potter and the Goblet of Fire*, Harry's loss underlies some of the most powerful scenes in Rowling's series. Regardless of our age when it happens, most of us feel a bit orphaned by the death of a parent, as perhaps Rowling did. At the very least, Anne Rowling's premature death suggests the degree to which Harry's emotional experience echoes Joanne's.

Becoming a Single Mother and an Author

Attempting to recover from her mother's death, Rowling moved in 1991 to Oporto, Portugal to teach English as a foreign language ("A Rowling Timeline"). On the backs of lesson plans or on scraps of paper during a free moment, she scratched down notes, invented names, and plotted the narrative for the *Harry Potter* series. Acutely aware of names, Rowling (pronounced "rolling") recalls her students making jokes about her name, but instead of using "rolling pin" as her peers did when she was a child, the Portuguese pupils said "Rolling Stone" ("Not Especially"). Student taunts aside, she enjoyed teaching En-glish in her afternoons and evenings while writing in the mornings. Determined to start the series off well, she wrote 10 different first chapters for *Harry Potter and the Philosopher's Stone* before finding the one she liked.

In 1992, she met Portuguese journalist Jorge Arantes. They discussed literature in cafés, fell in love, and after a brief romance, married in October. In July of the following year, Rowling gave birth to

Jessica, named for activist Jessica Mitford, whose courage and "total lack of self-pity" were qualities Rowling admired—and would soon need. After Jessica's birth, Rowling realized she had fallen out of love with Arantes. On November 17, she told him about her change in feelings, and he forced her to leave. Returning with the police the following day, she retrieved Jessica, a few belongings, all her *Harry Potter* notes, and three complete chapters of *Harry Potter and the Philosopher's Stone*. In late 1993, with Jessica and her luggage in tow, she returned to Great Britain, deciding to live in Edinburgh, Scotland, near her sister and brother-in-law. An unemployed single mother at twenty-eight, Joanne Rowling found herself living on public assistance.

Just as she was returning to England, John Major's ruling Tory party was unveiling a "back to basics" campaign, calling for a "return" to a mythical, idyllic 1950s Britain—and blaming single mothers for social ills. Angry at opportunistic politicians and depressed over the failure of her marriage, Rowling decided to use her time on the dole to finish the first *Harry Potter* novel, which even then she saw as the first in a seven-book series. She never believed that writing the book would make her rich, and she doubted that she would even find a publisher. Instead, she felt it was something that she simply had to do. Rowling later remarked that writing the "book saved my sanity. [. . .] I've never been more broke and the little I had saved went on baby gear. In the wake of my marriage, having worked all my life, I was suddenly an unemployed single parent in a grotty little flat. The manuscript was the only thing I had going for me" (Johnstone, "Happy ending").

Actually, the manuscript and her friends were all she had going for her. It's no coincidence that Rowling identifies with Harry's "close relationship with his friends" and believes that she would be lost without her friends ("JK Rowling Chat"). Her old friend Séan Harris lent her money for the deposit on the flat, and Di's husband had recently opened Nicolson's Restaurant, where Joanne sat and wrote for hours, nursing a cold cup of coffee while her daughter slept. She also pursued a teaching certificate so that she could attain a job as a French teacher, but even as she worked toward this goal, she often used the college's computers to work on her manuscript instead of her homework. "I set myself a deadline; I would finish the Harry novel before starting work as a French teacher, and try to get it published" ("Not Especially").

These were difficult years for Jo Rowling, anxious about being able to support her daughter and sometimes even denying herself food so that Jessica would have enough. "For a few years there, I really worried about money. I lived with it like there was a person living with me," Rowling recalls (Treneman, "Harry and Me"). The depression she endured during these years finds its imaginative expression in Dementors, the hooded creatures who "drain peace, hope and happiness out of the air around them." As Professor Lupin tells Harry in *Harry Potter and the Prisoner of Azkaban*, "Get too near a Dementor and every good feeling, every happy memory will be sucked out of you" (140). Fortunately, Rowling's sister and restless creativity sustained her as she continued to write, drawing inspiration from a variety of sources. Though she of course did not try its remedies on herself, *Culpeper's Complete Herbal* was a lucky find for Rowling during her years of inventing Harry's story. Written by Nicholas Culpeper in the seventeenth century and still in print, the book inspired names for potion ingredients, Professor Flitwick's plants, and even character names. As she worked on finishing *Harry Potter and the Philosopher's Stone*, Rowling told the story to Di, the first person to hear Harry's tale. Di liked it. Encouraged by her sister's response, Rowling applied for and won an £8,000 grant from the Scottish Arts Council. Supported by this money, she continued amassing notes for the planned *Harry Potter* series and finished the first book in 1995.

Harry Potter and the Publishers

While working as a French teacher at Leith Academy "and being serenaded down the corridors with the first line of the theme from Rawhide ('Rolling, rolling, rolling, keep those wagons rolling . . .')" ("Not Especially"), Rowling sought a publisher for *Harry Potter and the Philosopher's Stone*. After one publisher sent it back, she went to the library, where looking at a list of agents in *Artists' and Writers' Yearbook*, she decided to send her manuscript to two, one of whom—Christopher Little—she chose because she liked his name. It landed in his "slush pile" of unsolicited manuscripts, but two days later, Little happened to pick it up on the way to lunch with someone. That person was late, and as Little began reading about Harry, he says, "my toes curled" (Stahl). After lunch, he wrote to tell Rowling that he would represent her. Upon receiving an envelope from him, she assumed it contained a rejection note. Opening it, she found a letter saying, "Thank you. We would be pleased to receive the balance of your manuscript on an exclusive basis." As she remembers, "It was the best letter of my life. I read it eight times" (Glaister). Little began seeking a publisher, but Penguin, TransWorld, and Harper-Collins all turned down the manuscript, claiming that its 120,000-word length was too long for a children's novel (Macdonald 9). However, by late 1996, Little had sold the rights to Bloomsbury for £2,000 (Rustin). This money, combined with the grant from the Scottish Arts Council, enabled Rowling to quit her job and fulfill her life's dream of writing full-time.

A month after Bloomsbury published the first Harry Potter novel, Little called Rowling to tell her that an auction was taking place. She thought, "An auction? [. . .] Sotheby's? Christie's Antiques? What IS he on about?" (Carey). Speaking at about 8 PM Edinburgh time, Little explained that American publishers were bidding for her book, and the price was up to five figures. When Little called back two hours later, it was up to six figures (Weir). "That was amazing," she says. "I was like Elizabeth Bennett, you know, 'She *knew*, rather than *felt* she was happy'" (Carey).[4] Arthur A. Levine of Scholastic outbid Hyperion, Putnam, and Random House, paying $105,000 for the manuscript (Cowell). Levine says that what he loved most about the first Harry Potter novel was "the idea of growing up unappreciated, feeling outcast and then this great satisfaction of being discovered" (Levine and Carvajal).

During the next several years, Rowling would move rapidly from the great satisfaction of being discovered to becoming the most popular author in the world. She gained fame as "J. K. Rowling," not as Joanne Rowling, because of her British publisher's marketing team. About two months before *Harry Potter and the Philosopher's Stone* was published in Great Britain, Bloomsbury asked if she wouldn't mind using her initials on the cover. She admits, "I would have let them call me Enid Snodgrass if they published the book," but she still wondered why. When she asked, she learned Bloomsbury thought that "J. K. Rowling" would look more striking than "Joanne Rowling." So, Rowling asked, "Why? *Really?*" Her publisher confessed, "Well, we think boys will like this book, but we're not sure that they'll pick it up if a woman wrote it" (National Press Club). The gender of the author did not remain secret for long, however. Published in June 1997, *Harry Potter and the Philosopher's Stone* attracted readers of all ages, rose to the top of the British bestseller lists, and within a few months, "J. K." appeared on television to receive the Smarties Book Prize (not "wearing a false beard," Rowling wryly observes [National Press Club]). When the second Harry Potter novel was published in July of the following year, it received strong reviews and brisk sales. In September, Scholastic published the first novel in the United States (as *Harry Potter and the Sorcerer's Stone.*) In October, Rowling traveled to the United States for the first time, embarking upon a ten-day book tour. She was elated by children's enthusiasm for her work and surprised that many children, unable to wait for *Harry Potter and the Chamber of Secrets* to be published in the United States, had bought it from British booksellers via the Internet (Walker, "Edinburgh author"). In December, the book began its ascent up the *New York Times* list of hardcover bestsellers.

Pottermania

In 1999, Rowling became a superstar and Harry Potter an international phenomenon. In January, not yet a celebrity in America, she embarked upon a three-week U.S. book tour, surprised at her good fortune. When she returned later in the year to promote *Harry Potter and the Prisoner of Azkaban*, huge crowds greeted her, and the press compared the public's response to the Beatles' U.S. tours, dubbing Rowling's tour "Pottermania." Amidst traveling back and forth to America, she was writing the fourth novel, then titled *Harry Potter and the Doomspell Tournament*, which—when published—raised her public profile to the level of pop stars, prime ministers, and presidents. Uncomfortable with the idea of being a celebrity, Rowling was even more unnerved when members of the press began showing up on her doorstep. It is tempting to see *Harry Potter and the Goblet of Fire*'s Rita Skeeter as a response to the tabloid press. As Hermione shouts at Skeeter, "you don't care do you, anything for a story, and anyone will do, won't they?" (391). Rowling claims "Rita Skeeter [. . .] was always planned," but she adds, "I think I enjoyed writing her a bit more than I would have done if I hadn't met a lot of journalists, though!"

Though she decided not to mount a large book-signing tour in support of *Goblet of Fire*, Rowling did consent to a few readings, such as the one she did in Toronto, Canada, on October 22, when she and Canadian authors Ken Oppel and Tim Wynne-Jones addressed a crowd of 15,000 at the SkyDome as part of the International Festival of Authors at Harbourfront Centre. Apprehensive before a crowd of this size, she joked, "I feel like I should be leading you all into revolution" (Egan). Her decision to visit Toronto, specifically, derived in part from the organizers' promise to keep the ticket prices low enough for children to attend and in part from her friendship with a Toronto-area family. In July 1999, nine-year-old Natalie McDonald, a Harry Potter fan dying of leukemia, sent a letter that arrived just after Rowling had gone on a two-week vacation. When she returned, Rowling quickly sent e-mails to Natalie and her mother, Valerie. Although Natalie died the day before, Joanne and Valerie struck up a correspondence, and as a tribute to Valerie's daughter, the Sorting Hat sends Natalie McDonald to Gryffindor, making Natalie the only "real" person to appear so far in the *Harry Potter* series (*Goblet of Fire* 159). Apart from events like readings in Great Britain, naming her favorite music on Radio Four's "Desert Island Discs," and breakfast in New York with the ten winners of Scholastic's "How Harry Potter changed my life" contest (which drew 10,000 entries), Rowling has limited her public appearances, preferring to remain at home with her daughter and to work on the fifth novel, tentatively titled *Harry Potter and the Order of the Phoenix*.

In recognition of her achievement, Rowling received an OBE (Order of the British Empire) in June 2000. That same month, she received a Doctor of Letters from the University of St Andrews, and in July, her alma mater, the University of Exeter, awarded her a Doctor of Letters because "what she writes makes the world a better place," explained Exeter professor Peter Wiseman ("Now it's Doctor Rowling"). Though happiest when writing, Rowling has been using her celebrity to help make the world a better place. In 2000, she donated £500,000 to Britain's National Council for One Parent Families and, in December of the same year, made her first speech as its ambassador. Rowling criticized the "back to basics" message promoted by former Prime Minister John Major when she was a struggling single mother, and she rejected Shadow Home Secretary Ann Widdecombe's argument that society should adopt the two-parent, heterosexual model as the "preferred norm." Observing that a quarter of Britain's children were being raised by single parents, Rowling said, "We may not be some people's preferred norm, but we are here." Echoing the words of Sirius Black in chapter 27 of *Harry Potter and the Goblet of Fire*, she added, "We should judge how civilised a society is not by what it prefers to call normal, but by how it treats its most vulnerable members." In any case, "When you take poverty out of the equation, the vast majority of children from one-parent families do just as well as children from couple families" (Judge). She also wrote the foreword to the Council's *Families Just Like Us*, a pamphlet for—in Rowling's words—"any parent who is looking for children's books that reflect and celebrate the fact that families come in many different shapes and sizes" (1).

With proceeds to go to Comic Relief U.K., an organization devoted to helping children in the poorest countries of the world, Rowling wrote two of the books that appear in the *Harry Potter* novels: *Fantastic Beasts and Where to Find Them* by Newt Scamander, and *Quidditch Through the Ages* by Kennilworthy Whisp. So that the books generate as much money as possible for Comic Relief, printers and booksellers either donated their work or agreed to take less than their usual profits, and publications like *USA Today* and the *New York Times* donated advertising space. The £22 million that Rowling's books are expected to raise will provide money for AIDS education, help to unite families separated by war, and contribute to other good works. Published in March 2001, the "spinoff" books indicate how fully Rowling has imagined this magical world, display her great gift for satire, and give fans something to read while they await the fifth installment.

2

The Novels

"**W**hy are the books so popular?" is the question that J. K. Rowling gets asked most frequently. Her reply? "I don't want to analyze that. I don't want to decide that there's a formula [. . .] because I want to carry on writing them the way I want to write them and not, you know, put ingredient X in there." She concludes, "It's for other people to decide that, not me" (National Press Club). One reason this question may seem so difficult to answer is that the *Harry Potter* novels represent the creative synthesis of a lifetime of reading, and Rowling is very widely read. Another reason is that the books operate on many levels, with many layers of meaning. To tease out those influences and to examine closely some of those layers, this chapter examines the many levels on which the books operate and looks at the many genres in which one might place this series.

Education: Tom, Alice, and Harry

Though Rowling does not include school novels among her favorites, one genre from which the *Harry Potter* novels borrow is the boarding-school novel, of which Thomas Hughes's *Tom Brown's School-days* (1857) is considered the progenitor. Rowling's series is hardly *Harry Potter's Schooldays*, but Hogwarts under Albus Dumbledore, like Rugby under Thomas Arnold, seeks to provide its students not only with knowledge but also with a moral education. What the characters learn inside the classroom is as important as what they learn outside of it. Dumbledore, Harry realizes in the final chapter of *Philospher's Stone*, knew that he, Ron, and Hermione would try to reach and to protect the Philosopher's Stone, and "instead of stopping us, he taught us just enough to help" (219). In smaller ways, just as it takes courage for Tom Brown to stand up to Flashman, so Harry shows his moral fiber by standing up to the Hogwarts bully Draco Malfoy, and as Tom excels at football and cricket, so Harry excels at Quidditch. However, beyond these generic similarities, the comparisons break down. *Harry Potter* may be a moral series, and the central role of Quidditch suggests the importance of physical education. However, Rowling's co-educational Hogwarts is a far cry from the "muscular Christianity" of Thomas Hughes's all-boys Rugby. Where Hughes's narrator is given to lecturing the reader, Rowling's narrator generally lets the story deliver its morals without intervening—the notable exception being Dumbledore, who at the end of each book steps in to offer some moral conclusion. Though both main characters grow through their friendships, Harry Potter's friends seem more central than Harry East and George Arthur. Harry is clearly the star of the series, but these novels have nearly as much to say about the development of Ron Weasley and Hermione Granger.

Harry and Ron get into trouble with some regularity, but the novels rarely celebrate mischief for its own sake (as many schoolboy novels do). The mischievous side of Tom Brown and Harry East finds full expression in characters like Richmal Crompton's William, Frank Richards's Billy Bunter, Anthony Buckeridge's Jennings, and

Geoffrey Willans and Ronald Searle's Molesworth. However, the naughty schoolchildren in the Harry Potter novels are Fred and George Weasley; they are *not* the central characters. In fact, Hermione, who is every bit as good a friend to Harry as Ron, has an overdeveloped sense of fealty to the rules. Her character shows that rule-breaking is not always the right thing to do, as when she advises Harry and Ron not to meet Malfoy and Crabbe for the midnight duel. Not only do they risk losing points for Gryffindor, but they walk right into the trap Malfoy set for them: he never intended to show up for the duel, hoping that Harry and Ron would, getting themselves caught by Filch and Mrs. Norris. If Ron and Harry's growing recognition of the importance of some rules and laws owes much to Hermione's influence, it can equally be said that her increasing willingness to judge which laws are just and which are unjust reflects the beneficial influence that Ron and Harry have on her. The books do not glorify rule-breaking for its own sake but, rather, ask the reader to contemplate the reasons behind the rule-breaking.

The *Harry Potter* books do offer moral lessons, but Rowling's vision of education has clearer parallels to that of Lewis Carroll's. (And, given Rowling's early story about her sister falling down a rabbit hole, Rowling appears to have been familiar with Alice from quite a young age.) At once playful and serious, the best lessons of Hogwarts offer what—to judge by Carroll's critiques in the *Alice* novels—a traditional Victorian education lacked and what remains absent from dull classes today. Alice retains little useful information from her lessons, because she has been taught to memorize but never to ask questions or to think about what she has learned. In *Alice in Wonderland* (1865), she recalls "saying lessons, and began to repeat" a rhyme (23) and, later, after thinking "How the creatures order one about, and make one repeat lessons," Alice decides that she "may as well be at school at once" (106). As the Gryphon says, "That's the reason they're called lessons [. . .] because they lessen from day to day" (99). Rowling mocks this learning-by-rote process in the character of Professor Binns, whose name echoes "dustbins" (a humorous way of implying that his lessons are "rubbish") and who lectures his students, droning on and on, as they struggle to remain awake and to take notes. Binns is reputed to have fallen asleep in the staffroom, died, and "got up the next morning to teach, leaving his body behind him"; appropriately, he teaches History of Magic, "the only class taught by a ghost" (*Philospher's Stone* 99). Just as the Mouse's very "dry" history lesson in chapter 3 of *Alice in Wonderland* would be terribly boring if the animals did not interrupt with questions, so Binns's class is only interesting on the one day in which the class does get to ask questions. When, in *Harry Potter and the Chamber of Secrets*, Hermione asks Binns about the Chamber of Secrets, he is "completely thrown by such an unusual show of interest" but answers anyway, and the class listens, hanging on his every word and asking questions (114).

Numbers, Names, Character, Games

Inasmuch as Rowling's model of education can be aligned with Carroll's, the advice seems to be, first, that students learn only when they not only memorize but also put their knowledge to use and, second, that learning should be fun. Like Alice in Carroll's books and the title character in Diana Wynne Jones' *The Lives of Christopher Chant*, students in the well-taught classes of Hogwarts learn best by doing: Professor Lupin gives them hands-on practice at warding off magical creatures; Professor Moody puts them through their paces by forcing them to ward off curses. As the narrative voice (closely aligned with Chant) remarks in Jones's novel, "he really liked [. . .] working magic that actually did something. [. . .] That made it far more interesting than the silly things he had tried to learn at school" (92).

In the books of Jones, Carroll, and Rowling, joy in learning finds expression through games with words, numbers, and ideas. Sharing Carroll's affection for puzzles and games ("Why is a raven like a writing-desk?"), Rowling offers a logical puzzle at the end of book 1, the anagram "Tom Marvolo Riddle" in book 2, and the Sphinx's riddle in the Third Task of book 4.[5] Some of Carroll's games appear to have inspired Rowling's directly: chess sets with living pieces (as well as the life-size chessmen at the end of *Philosopher's Stone*) recall those in *Through the Looking-Glass and What Alice Found There* (1872), and letters addressed to "*Mr. H. Potter / The Cupboard under the Stairs / 4 Privet Drive / Little Whinging / Surrey*" bring to mind the letter addressed to "*Alice's Right Foot, Esq / Hearthrug / near the Fender / (with Alice's love)*" in *Alice in Wonderland*. Even the Mirror of Erised's name ("Erised" is "desirE" spelled backward) may have its antecedent in *Through the Looking Glass*.[6] However, most of Rowling's games lack such an apparently immediate influence, and they suggest instead an intellectual playfulness characteristic of not only Carroll but also Norton Juster.

The scope for the imagination—to borrow the phrase of L. M. Montgomery's Anne Shirley, another literary orphan—evident in Juster's *The Phantom Tollbooth* (1961) and Carroll's *Alice* books animates Rowling's work, albeit in a more understated fashion. Though chapters 14, 15, and 16 of *The Phantom Tollbooth* compel Milo to use his math skills, Rowling gently weaves the theme of mathematics through the "Diagon Alley" chapter of *Harry Potter and the Philosopher's Stone*. After the mathematical clue ("diagonally") in the chapter's title, Rowling populates much of the chapter with prime numbers. The wizarding monetary system relies on primes—"Seventeen silver Sickles to a Galleon and twenty-nine Knuts to a Sickle," as Hagrid explains (58). Both 17 and 29 are primes. James Potter used an 11-inch wand, Harry's wand is 11 inches long, he pays "seven gold Galleons" for it, and he gives the owl "five Knuts" for delivering a letter (63, 65, 50). Eleven, seven, and five are prime numbers, and both seven Galleons and five Knuts produce the products of prime numbers. This is interesting primarily because Hagrid retrieves the philosopher's stone from vault 713 of Gringott's Wizards' bank, and 713 is the product of two primes, 23 and 31.[7] Given that some consider prime numbers to be mystical, the chapter's numerical symbolism subtly introduces the novel's themes of magic and the supernatural. When discussing the fact that there will be seven books in the series, Rowling observed, "Seven is a magical number, a mystical number" (Mehren).

Details like the play with numbers in Diagon Alley may elude readers during their first trip through the books, because the novels are so driven by plot. However, these are allusive works that reward serious readers and rereaders of all ages. It's no accident that Harry, Ron, and Hermione spend a lot of time in the library: to judge by her imaginative resources, Rowling has spent a lot of time in the library herself. The names alone reveal the many levels on which her stories are operating. Alison Lurie believes that Harry's name "suggests not only craftsmanship but both English literature and English history: Shakespeare's Prince Hal and Harry Hotspur, the brave, charming, impulsive heroes of *Henry IV*; and Beatrix Potter, who created that other charming and impulsive classic hero, Peter Rabbit." As Lurie's comment reveals, the names resonate in many different directions. The well-read might notice that Mrs. Norris, Filch's snooping cat, has borrowed her name from Fanny's nasty, bossy aunt in Jane Austen's *Mansfield Park* (1814), or that Hermione shares a name with the character who, in Shakespeare's *The Winter's Tale* (1610–1611), is thought dead until what appears to be her statue comes to life. The philologist may note that Albus Dumbledore, the Hogwarts Headmaster, has a first name meaning wisdom or whiteness and a surname that is Old English for bumblebee. Those with a knowledge of Christianity should recognize Hedwig, Harry's owl, as being named for a medieval saint. Poppy, the first name of infirmary matron Madam Pomfrey, may be a reference to the flower that, when condensed, becomes opium, the narcotic once used to relieve pain and to soothe the sick. Yet, failing to notice that (for example) Professor Vector, Hermione's Arithmancy professor, is named for a mathematical term does not diminish the enjoyment of *Harry Potter and the Goblet of Fire*. Rather, rich with imaginative detail and full of allusions, the *Harry Potter* novels can only be appreciated fully on subsequent readings.

In *Fantastic Beasts and Where to Find Them* and especially in *Quidditch Through the Ages*, the two pseudonymous schoolbooks, Rowling displays an inventiveness on par with Carroll, Juster, P. L. Travers, Edward Lear, or Dr. Seuss. The Harry Potter novels, too, bubble with the intensely imaginative ideas that are characteristic of works by these authors, yet in these books, Rowling's word-play seems almost incidental—delightful touches, left in the background, perhaps to remind us of the extent to which she has imagined the world of her characters. She does not dwell on Bertie Bott's Every Flavor Beans (which, in addition to the usual flavors, also offer beans that taste like tripe, liver, or earwax), on talking chess pieces, or on pictures with subjects who move. Just as characters in fairy tales are not surprised when a wolf talks or a frog turns into a prince, Rowling offers a matter-of-fact fantasy, in which magic is so thoroughly part of the landscape that it's taken for granted. Of course, while we or even the characters might take such magical items for granted, she never does, carefully altering them to suit the plot. In *Harry Potter and the Goblet of Fire*, which opens with gossip in a local pub, the subjects of portraits move from frame to frame—gossiping. During the holiday festivities, those portraits get a bit tipsy, and after the castle has been cleaned up for visiting students, the pictures chafe at the scrubbing and are grumpy when their skin feels raw because of it. When the narrative takes a darker turn in *Harry Potter and the Prisoner of*

Azkaban, the Fat Lady in the portrait at the entrance to Gryffindor tower briefly becomes central to the plot when Sirius's knife slashes her. Even when the Fat Lady or Sir Cadogan do move to the foreground, however, Rowling's magical inventions do not upstage the main characters. She never seems to be showing off or throwing out ideas for their own sake. The Omnioculars, the Pensieve, the Time-Turner, and the living portraits all deftly advance the story, reminding us that Rowling's plots are always grounded in character, not gimmicks.

Characterization in the *Harry Potter* books combines elements of psychological realism, caricature, and melodrama. Minor characters like Stan Shunpike and Ernie Prang certainly owe the most to caricature, but Rowling's creations usually do not fit neatly into any single category. If the villains seem melodramatic, then look a bit more closely. Many of Voldemort's lines in *Harry Potter and the Goblet of Fire* go beyond conventional melodrama, playfully indulging in melodramatic kitsch. Voldemort even evinces a sense of humor, as when, recounting the need for "three powerful ingredients" that assisted him in his rebirth, he quips, "Well, one of them was already at hand, was it not, Wormtail? Flesh given by a servant" (569). His pun on "at hand" winks at the knowledge that not only is Wormtail at hand, but Wormtail's hand is the flesh that helped to restore Voldemort to his body. To prevent Voldemort from remaining a campy caricature, Rowling has told us about his childhood, school days, and patricide. His inner life—rejected by his father, raised in an orphanage—makes Voldemort almost sympathetic. Snape, another villainous sort, bears an unfortunate resemblance to the stereotype of the Jew: cunning, greasy-haired, and sallow-skinned, he sputters with rage and threatens to poison not only Neville's toad but Harry himself. Yet, Snape's school days and work as a double agent combine with Dumbledore's trust to make him one of the most intriguing characters in the series. The heroes and heroines receive the most detailed inner lives, of course. However, though we know far more about Harry, Ron, and Hermione than anyone else, Rowling offers glimpses into Moaning Myrtle's life before death, Hagrid's adolescence, and Neville's childhood. The sad tale of the Longbottoms' madness, revealed in *Harry Potter and the Goblet of Fire*, makes it much harder to view Neville as purely the figure of fun he at first seemed to be. Neville has suffered, as Harry realizes when he imagines "how it must feel to have parents still living, but unable to recognize you." Though Harry "often got sympathy from strangers for being an orphan," he decides "that Neville deserved it [sympathy] more than he did" (527).

Like Roald Dahl's James Henry Trotter or Charles Dickens's Oliver Twist and David Copperfield, Harry Potter is marked by early tragedy and forced to live with cruel, surrogate parents. Vernon and Petunia Dursley, the aunt and uncle who raise Harry, bear a striking resemblance to Mr. and Mrs. Wormwood in Dahl's *Matilda* (1988), but Harry's beginnings even more closely echo those of James Trotter in Dahl's *James and the Giant Peach* (1961). Orphaned at four years old when angry rhinos escape from the zoo and trample both his parents, James is raised by Aunt Sponge and Aunt Spiker, two "really horrible people" who force their nephew to live in a room "as bare as a prison cell" (2). Harry, orphaned at about a year old when both his parents are simultaneously killed, lives with a horrible aunt and uncle, who make him live under the stairs. As in the development of James Trotter and David Copperfield, Harry's early life engenders in him a degree of self-doubt that makes him sympathetic and gives him room to grow more confident as he recognizes his abilities. Indicative of his deep-seated worries, Harry, at the end of the second chapter of *Chamber of Secrets*, has a dream that seems inspired by Kafka's "A Hunger Artist" (1924): "He dreamed that he was on show in a zoo, with a card reading 'Under-age Wizard' attached to his cage. People goggled through the bars at him as he lay, starving and weak, on a bed of straw" (*Chamber of Secrets* 22). In the scene that follows, Fred, George, and Ron will rescue him from imprisonment at the Dursleys, and in the rest of the novel, Harry will again prove himself at Hogwarts. In all of the novels, however, his highly developed awareness of what can go wrong endears him to us.

Fantasy, Mystery, and Ambiguity

Another aspect of Harry's appeal is that of the apparently ordinary child who turns out to be special—which, surely, is a secret wish of many children. As Rowling has said, "I was aware when I was writing that this was a very common fantasy for children: 'These boring people cannot be my parents. They just can't be. I'm so much more special than that'" (Phillips). Like Taran in Lloyd Alexander's chronicles of Prydain (1964–1968), Will Stanton in Susan Cooper's *Dark Is Rising* series (1965–1977), and Lyra Silvertongue in Philip Pullman's *His Dark Materials* trilogy (1995–2000), Harry is special. And, like the children all these books, he's on a mission. Though Rowling claims that fantasy is her least favorite genre (she prefers the realism of Roddy Doyle), her books owe a lot to the traditions of fantasy. Harry, a classic fantasy hero, is the oppressed child who fights back, proving himself and quashing his enemies. Featuring more than 100 characters, the *Harry Potter* series is an epic fantasy. Though we have only the first four novels by which to judge it, the series has every indication of leading toward a *Last Battle*—to borrow the title of the final Narnia novel—in which the forces of good vanquish the forces of evil.

While they attain the magical skills they will need in the confrontation toward which the narrative pushes them, a fantasy novel's young characters embark on a journey of self-discovery. As does Bilbo

Baggins in J. R. R. Tolkien's *The Hobbit* (1937) and Ged in Ursula K. Le Guin's *A Wizard of Earthsea* (1968), Harry Potter gains a deeper understanding of himself as he moves toward the anticipated final battle. Initially worried that his Muggle upbringing will place him at a disadvantage among Hogwarts students, Harry discovers that he does have talents: he's great at flying and a natural Seeker on his house's Quidditch team. Just as we all must come to terms with who we are, Harry also wonders if some of his abilities make him a bad person. A Parselmouth, Harry can talk to snakes, a rare ability he shares with dark wizards like Voldemort and Salazar Slytherin. Possessing the capacity to speak Parseltongue worries Harry, because the Sorting Hat had offered to place him in Slytherin, only sending him to Gryffindor when he kept chanting "Not Slytherin, not Slytherin" (*Philosopher's Stone* 90–91). When he expresses this anxiety, Dumbledore advises, "It is our choices, Harry, that show us what we truly are, far more than our abilities" (*Chamber of Secrets* 245). Dumbledore's moral applies equally well to Ron and Hermione, who also come into their own during the course of the series. At first an overbearing school swot, Hermione grows more comfortable with herself, develops a strong sense of commitment to her friends, and — though she remains the smartest student in her year — learns to resist the impulse to display her intelligence at every available opportunity. Ron has thus far developed less than Hermione or Harry, but he is gradually emerging from the shadow of his older brothers, playing a key role in solving the mysteries of the first three novels and sharing some of Harry's limelight in *Goblet of Fire*.

As in many fantasy novels and fairy tales, the central character is on a quest; however, the narrative of Harry's quest unfolds more like a classic mystery. In the first novel, Harry seeks to protect the Philosopher's Stone; in the second, to stop the basilisk from attacking students; in the third, to elude and to be revenged upon Sirius Black, whom he believes was an accomplice in his parents' murder; and in the fourth, to win the Triwizard Tournament cup. In its effort to highlight Harry's quests, the previous sentence over-simplifies all four novels. Ron and Hermione often join in Harry's quests, and the implicit and explicit nature of each quest changes as Rowling's mystery unfolds. In *Harry Potter and the Philosopher's Stone*, the three characters first wonder what is hidden on the right-hand side of the third-floor corridor; upon learning what it is, they puzzle over who wants it, suspect Snape, and finally decide to protect it themselves. Concurrent with this mystery quest, they also want to know: Who is Nicolas Flamel? Who or what has been attacking the unicorns? Why did Snape seem to be sabotaging Harry's broom at the Quidditch match? At the opening banquet, why did Harry's scar hurt when Snape appeared to be looking at him? Of course, two overriding questions in all of the novels are: How did Harry survive the Avada Kevadra curse that killed both of his parents? And why did Voldemort want to kill Harry in the first place? Harry asks Dumbledore both questions in *Philosopher's Stone*. The Hogwarts headmaster provides a partial answer to the first question when he says that Harry's mother died to save him, and that Voldemort cannot understand a love that powerful. In words that may echo the author's sentiments toward her own late mother, Dumbledore tells Harry, "to have been loved so deeply, even though the person who loved us is gone, will give us some protection for ever" (216). However, Dumbledore does not tell us why Voldemort wanted the Potters dead; that mystery persists.

If the first novel appears to have many mystery plots going at once, it is remarkably simple when compared with the subsequent three. Each of the next three books grows more complex as its mysteries grow more intricate and clever. The final hundred or so pages of *Harry Potter and the Prisoner of Azkaban*—themselves as gripping and elaborate a conclusion to a mystery as one could hope for—prove only to foreshadow the complexity of *Harry Potter and the Gob-*

let of Fire. In the *Prisoner of Azkaban*'s concluding pages, we witness the arc of Rowling's narrative expanding—an expansion that continues in its sequel. Though the first two novels provide a sense of narrative closure, the next two offer only an emotional resolution, coupled with an uneasy feeling that the dangerous world beyond Hogwarts will continue to bear down upon the young characters. After realizing that their perceptions of several major characters were incorrect, Harry and Hermione listen in disbelief as Dumbledore tells them, "I have no power to make other men see the truth, or to overrule the Minister for Magic" (*Prisoner of Azkaban* 287). Then, in what can only be a reference to the endings of the previous two novels, Harry realizes that he "had grown used to the idea that Dumbledore could solve anything. He had expected Dumbledore to pull some amazing solution out of the air. But no . . . their last hope was gone" (288). We readers had grown used to the idea that Dumbledore could set things right, too. *Harry Potter and the Goblet of Fire* complicates matters further, revealing corruption in government ministries, the possibilities for global misunderstanding, and the alliance in disarray while Voldemort returns to power.

Underscoring their complexity, the novels view official systems of power skeptically, placing greater faith in unofficial alliances. While not all bureaucrats are corrupt, many officials appear bumbling, misguided, or acting in their own self-interest instead of for the public good. Though Arthur Weasley is kind-hearted and works hard in the Misuse of Muggle Artefacts Office, Ludo Bagman pays more attention to gambling than running the Department of Games and Sports, Cornelius Fudge tends to fudge things (as his name suggests) as Minister for Magic, and Barty Crouch (the Minister for International Magical Co-operation) is more concerned with appearing correct than with being honest or just. Tellingly, when Crouch was head of the Department of Magical Law Enforcement, he sent the innocent Sirius Black to Azkaban without a trial. Unlike the criminal justice system and other official channels of power, the alliance that Dumbledore begins to reassemble in the penultimate chapter of *Harry Potter and the Goblet of Fire* holds more promise. Rowling evinces trust in the greater efficacy of *ad hoc* groups throughout the novels. When school officials either ignore them (*Philosopher's Stone*) or fail to solve the problem (*Chamber of Secrets*), Harry, Ron, and Hermione form their own alliance and solve the problem themselves. Rowling seems more comfortable when power courses through unofficial networks—as if its activist spirit is more demo-cratic than power entrenched in official channels. No stranger to political activism herself, Rowling implies that activists are more worthy of our trust than public officials are.

As the series develops, it grows increasingly interested in questions of power: who has it, who has the right to exercise it over another, who has the moral authority to wield it, and how it should be exercised. Perhaps the most striking example occurs during the nineteenth chapter of *Prisoner of Azkaban*, when Harry intervenes to stop Black and Lupin from killing Pettigrew, the man directly responsible for Voldemort killing Harry's parents. This moment of moral decision-making gives both readers and characters pause: Sirius asks Harry if he's sure, and when Harry explains why he is, he displays a quiet heroism. Harry saves Pettigrew because he does not think his father would want his best friends to become killers (275). Wonderfully, Harry both regrets his noble decision and receives high praise for it. When Pettigrew escapes, Harry accuses himself of helping Voldemort, albeit inadvertently. "I stopped Sirius and Professor Lupin killing Pettigrew! That makes it my fault, if Voldemort comes back!" Dumbledore quietly disagrees: "Hasn't your experience with the Time-Turner taught you anything, Harry? The consequences of our actions are always so complicated, so diverse, that predicting the future is a very difficult business indeed." In addition, Dumbledore notes that in saving Pettigrew, Harry has given Voldemort a deputy who is in Harry's debt. Dumbledore then adds gently, "I knew your father very well, both at Hogwarts and later [. . .]. He would have saved Pettigrew too, I am sure of it" (311). If Voldemort is interested in power for its own sake, Harry wishes to use his power only when it is *right* to do so. He could have had Pettigrew killed, avenging his parents' deaths, but sensing that vengeance is the wrong motive, he saves Pettigrew's life. In her *New Yorker* essay, Joan Acocella develops a fascinating analysis of power in Rowling's books, arguing that "Each of the novels approaches the problem from a different angle": the first novel is heroic; the second is "secular, topical, political"; the third is psychological; the fourth is more ambitious in its politics, introducing new topics (such as sex) but not yet answering the question of whether power is "reconcilable with goodness" (77–78).

Acocella's analysis reminds us that one of the most compelling aspects of these novels may be their ambiguity. During each novel, we wonder whether characters have done or are doing the right thing; at the end, many questions remain unanswered. During *Harry Potter and the Goblet of Fire*, we wonder if Ludo Bagman is aligned with the dark wizards or merely unscrupulous? At the end of the novel, we know him to be unscrupulous but not bad, though we do not know which side he will end up assisting. A character like Bagman could go either way. In *Prisoner of Azkaban*, after Harry overhears the "facts" (which turn out to be false) that Sirius Black betrayed his parents, we see Harry's dark side. He wants revenge on Black: but will he risk his own life trying to catch him? Harry decides not to, but the incident does call attention to some potential weaknesses that Voldemort could exploit. In future novels, will Harry be able to keep his temper under control? Will his strong resolve be an asset, a hindrance, or a bit of both? Perhaps the fact that these books raise as many questions as they answer accounts—at least in part—for their enormous appeal.

History and Ideology

George Orwell famously attributed the popularity of fiction for boys—among which he included boarding-school stories—to the need for working-class children to imagine themselves among the elite, and to the need for the elite to maintain their privileges by indoctrinating impressionable readers with the conservative values that (Orwell argued) these stories promoted. The "real function" of these tales, he wrote, "is to allow the boy who goes to a cheap private school (*not* a Council school) to feel that his school is just as 'posh' in the sight of God as Winchester or Eton" (480). While reading these tales at an impressionable age, Orwell argued, children indirectly absorb a conservative "set of beliefs"—"that the major problems of our time do not exist, that there is nothing wrong with *laissez-faire* capitalism, that foreigners are unimportant comics and that the British Empire is a sort of charity-concern which will last for ever" (483). Orwell's comments are intriguing in light of the worldwide popularity of Harry Potter. Hogwarts is an elite school, admitting only those with magical abilities *and*, presumably, whose names have been written down at the school since their birth, as Harry's was. (Knight Bus conductor Stan Shunpike and driver Ernie Prang do not appear to have attended Hogwarts; presumably, they were not admitted?) Despite the fact that only those who are born wizards or witches may attend Hogwarts, Rowling offers us many different types of students: the pale, hapless Neville Longbottom; the well-intentioned but swotty Hermione; Parvati and Padma Patil, evidently of Indian descent; Seamus Finnigan, who speaks with a strong Irish accent; and two black students, the dreadlocked Lee Jordan, a friend of George and Fred Weasley, and Angelina Johnson, Chaser for Gryffindor's Quidditch team. According to Orwell, school stories provide a variety of students with whom each type of reader can identify, increasing the reader's willingness to live vicariously through that character, feeling that his or her school is just as posh as Hog-warts (Orwell 469–470). If we accept Orwell's analysis, then perhaps the *Harry Potter* novels not only appeal to the desire to be among the elect but also mollify dissent against a system that depends upon birthright instead of merit.

The *Harry Potter* novels are not completely blind to the politics of class or race, however. The books not only side with the poorer Weasley family and oppose the elitist Malfoy family but also dis-play the effects that class-based privilege can have on the psyche. From the moment we first meet him, Ron Weasley is ashamed of his family's poverty. After complaining about his hand-me-down robes, wand, and rat, Ron almost tells Harry that his parents couldn't afford to buy him anything better than Scabbers, then interrupts himself and turns pink with embarrassment (*Philosopher's Stone* 75). When Harry sees the Weasley's house in the next book, Ron's first impulse is to apologize for it (*Chamber of Secrets* 29, 35–36). *Harry Potter and the Goblet of Fire* depicts the relationship between financial worth and self-worth even more vividly. In chap-ter 28, Ron is very upset when he learns that the leprechaun gold he had given Harry at the Quidditch World Cup has vanished, as all leprechaun gold does. "Must be nice," Ron says, "to have so much money you don't notice if a pocketful of Galleons goes miss-ing." After Harry encourages him to not to worry about it, Ron replies bitterly, "I hate being poor." Neither Harry nor Hermione know how to respond (474). Indeed, a sympathetic reading of Draco Malfoy would reveal that he, too, is damaged by his own class po-sition: his snobby behavior develops from being raised by a family that believes its unearned privileges of wealth and status depend entirely on merit. Though the books leave room for this interpre-tation, Rowling focuses more on how the subjects of Draco's taunts feel. Hermione counsels Ron to ignore Draco mocking him for be-ing poor, but being teased nonetheless hurts. Rowling, who herself endured privation while writing the first book, displays an acute awareness of classism's effects.

A critique of racism is much more central to the *Harry Potter* series than exploration of class prejudice. Though the use of names like Parvarti Patil and Cho Chang evinces an awareness of the many cultures that make up contemporary Britain, Rowling investigates the prejudices that develop around racial and cultural difference not through social realism but through fantasy. The *Harry Potter* novels expose prejudices in those who adhere to the belief system of Salazar Slytherin, a founding member of Hogwarts who believed that only children from "Pureblood" wizarding families should be allowed to attend. The moment that Malfoy calls Hermione a "filthy little Mudblood" in *Harry Potter and the Chamber of Secrets*, the scandalized reactions of the characters tell us that "Mudblood" is as offensive to them as "nigger" is to us (86). Lord Voldemort, the Malfoys, Harry's Aunt Marge, and all those who advocate hierarchies based on "natural" difference are *The Enemy* in Rowling's series. Rowling has even likened Voldemort's obsession with the lack of "purity" in his own blood—Voldemort's father was a Muggle, and his mother was a witch—to Adolf Hitler's mania for racial purity. The Dark Lord's zeal for Purebloods, she says, is "like Hitler and the Aryan ideal, to which he did not conform at all, himself. And so Voldemort is doing this also. He takes his own [perceived] inferiority, and turns it back on other people and attempts to exterminate in them what he hates in himself"(Solomon). Adding to the parallels between Nazis and evil forces in the *Harry Potter* books, the card bearing the Hogwarts headmaster's photo reveals that Dumbledore defeated a dark wizard in 1945, the year that World War II ended. When it seems as though a new war may be beginning near the end of *Harry Potter and the Goblet of Fire*, Dumbledore delivers several rousing speeches with distinctly Churchillian cadences.

Perhaps more significant to the treatment of bigotry in the novels is that Rowling does not merely demonize the bigots. The Dursleys, the Malfoys, Crabbe, Goyle, and Voldemort are unsympathetic characters, to be sure, but Rowling intimates that even apparently "good" characters harbor prejudices. As Dumbledore points out in the penultimate chapter of *Harry Potter and the Goblet of Fire*, Cornelius Fudge, though opposed to the methods of Voldemort's Death Eaters, nonetheless secretly believes that Pureblood wizards are superior to others (614–615). As a result, Harry finds himself rethinking his view of Fudge (613). Earlier in the same novel, when Harry and Ron overhear Hagrid admitting his giant ancestry, Ron's response displays a learned prejudice against giants (374). Though Ron recognizes the flaws in his reaction, Rita Skeeter's biased exposé of Hagrid reveals the extent of anti-giant sentiments in the magical community, just as the that hate mail Hermione receives shows just how many witches and wizards think Muggle-borns are inferior. Rowling's willingness to show that even "good" characters may think "Mudbloods" or giants are inferior illustrates that prejudice and hatred are not something that *other* people do. These are powerful beliefs embedded in the culture, which all of us absorb and know, even though we may not be conscious of ever having learned them. Rowling reveals this process of acculturation through those characters who, initially, are outsiders. Not having grown up within the wizarding community, Harry and Hermione are able to see the prejudices of the magical world much more clearly than Ron and many of his peers. Hermione and Harry know Hagrid as a friend first, so when Skeeter tries to taint him with the "sin" of giant parentage, they resist this cultural stereotype. Promoting peace and understanding between people from different backgrounds is not just the goal of the Triwizard Tournament—it's Rowling's goal, too.

So far, the house-elves confuse this message of inclusion, but whether the confusion is intentional on Rowling's part cannot yet be known. The house-elves speak in a pidgin dialect that borders on caricature, as in "Oh, you is a bad elf, Dobby!" (*Goblet of Fire* 332). On the other hand, Mr. Weasley expresses sympathy for the rights of house-elves, and Harry liberates Dobby, even if his response to Hermione's Society for the Promotion of Elfish Welfare is lukewarm at best. Hermione's earnest activism on behalf of the elves is harder to read: Rowling seems both to admire Hermione for her convictions and to mock her zeal as naïve or overdone. There are signs at the end of *Harry Potter and the Goblet of Fire* that the house-elf question may be resolved in later books. Dumbledore emphasizes that alliances between different groups will be important: he invites students of different nationalities to come to Hogwarts at any time, sends Hagrid and Madam Maxime as envoys to the giants, and uses rhetoric reminiscent of John F. Kennedy. Addressing the students of Hogwarts, Durmstrang, and Beauxbatons, Dumbledore says, "in the light of Voldemort's return, we are only as strong as we are united, as weak as we are divided," and "Differences of habit and language are nothing at all if our aims are identical and our hearts are open" (627). In light of Dumbledore's inspiring remarks, perhaps the house-elves, like the elves in J. R. R. Tolkien's *Lord of the Rings*, will form an important part of a wide-ranging alliance. Certainly, *all* of Orwell's criticisms of popular school stories do not apply to the *Harry Potter* series, though some of his comments may. For her part, when Rowling was asked if the racist, classist people she satirizes are "neo-Conservative or Thatcherite," she agreed that they were (Solomon).

Young Adults

Though hardly the gritty realism of Roddy Doyle's *The Woman Who Walked Into Doors* (1996) (which Rowling admires), Rowling's books do engage the real world. All the *Harry Potter* novels —

and especially the fourth, in which Harry and his peers enter adolescence—share some territory with the Young Adult Novel, over-
lapping with the work of writers like Jacqueline Wilson and Gillian
Cross. Like Andy in Wilson's *The Suitcase Kid* (1993) or Cassie in
Cross's *Wolf* (1990), Harry is a child with few adults to guide him,
a child who survives through his ability to adapt to new surround-
ings and to fashion his own unorthodox but effective family structure. As if to make this point, Rowling sometimes explicitly dra-
matizes Harry's need for parents. After he wakes up from a very
real nightmare, "What he really wanted (and it felt almost shame-
ful to admit it to himself) was someone like—someone like a *parent*: an adult wizard whose advice he could ask without feeling stupid, someone who cared about him" (*Goblet of Fire* 25). He then
writes to Sirius, who serves as a father-figure to Harry in *Goblet of
Fire*, even more so than Lupin had done in *Prisoner of Azkaban*.
The Weasleys, too, provide some of the familial support that Harry
would otherwise lack. Visiting the Weasleys are some of Harry's
happiest times, and, during the series, their family becomes his
own. They help send him off to school in all four novels, he spends
at least part of his summer holidays with them in three, and when
Mrs. Weasley comforts him near the end of *Goblet of Fire*, Harry
reflects that he "had no memory of ever being hugged like this, as
though by a mother" (620). In this sense, these novels are about
Harry creating his own surrogate family, composed of friends,
teachers, and sympathetic adults. Lacking biological parents, he
forges an alternate family structure.

In the Dursleys, Rowling offers a "traditional" family that, for all
its apparent normalcy, is much more unhealthy than Harry's non-
traditional familial network of peers and adults. As Rowling has said,
"My feelings about people who glorify 'the norm' are set down in
the first sentence of *Harry Potter and the Philosopher's Stone*: Mr.
and Mrs. Dursley of number four, Privet Drive, were proud to say

that they were perfectly normal, thank you very much" (Judge). If the Dursleys represent "the norm," then they illustrate the degree to which bourgeois values depend upon commodity culture. Like the Trottles in Eva Ibbotson's *The Secret of Platform 13* (1994), the Dursleys have been warped by their obsessive need to display their social status. Whether they are standing outside, loudly admiring Vernon Dursley's new company car "in very loud voices, so that the rest of the street would notice it, too," or indulging their greedy bully of a son, their belief system revolves around the idea that bigger is better, and that affluence is a moral good. Rowling delights in mocking the Dursleys during the opening chapters of each *Harry Potter* novel, and on a subtle level, Privet Drive—the Dursleys' address— takes its name from the shrub often grown as a hedge (which Harry is forced to trim in *Philosopher's Stone*) and is linked to both "Private" and "privy" (which can mean both "private" and "outhouse"). The name suggests a sly criticism of the Dursleys' faith in privacy and private property, but their massive son Dudley is a grotesque parody of their values. "I was told it would be politically incorrect to have a child so large," Rowling admits. "My response was that this was about abuse. It was abusive that the people around him are feeding him not only with their putrid ideas, but with food, like a goose. He's a victim of his parents"(Mehren). Though F. Anstey's *Vice Versa* (1882) is not a "Young Adult Novel" as such, both it and Rowling's Dursley family show how *not* to raise a child, delighting in punishing the parents (the father in Anstey, Harry's aunt and uncle in Rowling) for their failures.

If the Dursleys' relationships are warped because they depend upon exchange (as when Dudley is paid £20 for kissing his Aunt Marge Dursley), Harry's relationships are healthy because they depend upon genuine affection and lasting friendship. In *Philosopher's Stone*, Ron and Harry meet on the train, both feeling inadequate and apprehensive about going off to a new school, and they become fast friends. After the two confront a troll with Hermione, she becomes a friend, too. During the series, these three friends squabble with one another, give each other presents, argue, and come to one another's rescue. Their friendship is frequently tested, but it always endures. Ron and Harry refuse to talk to one another during several chapters of *Goblet of Fire*, and Ron and Hermione give each other the silent treatment for a similar length of time in *Prisoner of Azkaban*. Ultimately, however, they come round again, realizing that true friends are too important to be lost to stubbornness. As the trio of Harry, Ron, and Hermione grow up together, they enact a celebration of friendship, its ups and downs, its complexities, and finally, its strength. Gail A. Grynbaum, who reads the novels in terms of archetypal themes, suggests that these three may be a "central attraction of the series in these alienated times, a reminder to many readers who have felt alone since early childhood, of the lost archetype of comradeship" (24).

The Bildungsroman (German for "novel of formation"), like the Young Adult Novel, is about a protagonist's coming of age, and Rowling's *Harry Potter* series might be seen as a Bildungsroman divided into seven separate installments, one for each year of Harry's life. Unlike Enid Blyton's *Famous Five*, in which the children do not age, Harry and his friends grow up during a narrative that, if seen as one single and connected work, is roughly 1,500 pages long and counting.[8] Though we witness their childhoods largely through flashbacks, by the conclusion of the series Harry will have grown from a downtrodden, 10-year-old into (we presume) a mature 17-year-old. Midway through the Harry Potter epic, signs of their development have already begun. In *Prisoner of Azkaban*, Harry develops a crush on Cho Chang, and in *Goblet of Fire*, the Hogwarts students of Harry's year start to date one another, stumbling into adolescence. Ron and Hermione's relationship exemplifies teenage misunderstandings: they are obviously attracted to one another, but Ron has not yet realized it. In addition to grappling with overactive hormones, the characters also face increasingly serious problems and learn more about their roles in the world beyond Hogwarts. In the first novel, they successfully stop Voldemort from attaining the Philosopher's Stone and returning to power; in the fourth, they become part of a global alliance intended to prevent Voldemort—now restored to a human form—from gaining even more strength than he already has. Unlike the conclusion of *Philosopher's Stone*, success at the end of *Goblet of Fire* is far from assured. As Acocella has written, Rowling's great achievement "is that she asks her pre-teen readers to face the hardest questions of life, and does not shy away from the possibility that the answers may be sad: that loss may be permanent, evil ever-present, good exhaustible" (78).

The ability of the novels to deal with these hard questions reminds us that the *Harry Potter* series—like all good children's literature—is not *only* for children. As C. S. Lewis wrote, "I am almost inclined to set it up as a canon that a children's story which is enjoyed only by children is a bad children's story" (*Of This and Other Worlds* 59), and as Dr. Seuss said, "I never write for children. I write for people" (Cott). Rowling, too, has written the *Harry Potter* novels for people of all ages. The series has some obvious jokes for children, like "troll bogies" in *Philosopher's Stone*, the "Cockroach Cluster" candies in *Prisoner of Azkaban*, and Ron's remark, "Can I have a look at Uranus, too, Lavender?" in *Goblet of Fire*. However, there is much that even adult readers may miss, such as the fact that Fleur Delacour means "flower of the court" in French, that Minerva McGonagall shares her first name with the Roman goddess of wisdom, and the significance of Remus Lupin's name. Remus and his brother Romulus (legendary founders of Rome), both abandoned as infants, were raised by wolves; Lupin derives from the Latin *lupus*, meaning "wolf." When asked if she writes the books for children or adults, Rowling has said, "both. I wrote something that I knew I would like to read now, but I also wrote something that I knew I would like to have read at age 10" (National Press Club). Rowling understands that a good "children's" writer does not condescend to children, and she knows what goes unrecognized by those critics who turn up their noses at children's literature: adults carry their childhood experiences with them, and children understand a great deal more than most adults give them credit for. As C. S. Lewis wrote to a child correspondent, "I don't think age matters so much as people think. Parts of me are still 12 and I think other parts were already 50 when I was 12" (*Letters to Children* 34).

The age range of her audience and the wide range of genres synthesized by her imagination may confound the expectations of both readers and reviewers. Noticing the realistic strains, some may hope for the *Harry Potter* novels to offer more elements of social realism, or seizing upon the more fantastic elements, others might wonder why social issues like slavery and racism enter the series. However, to wish for a greater fidelity to a particular genre presumes that genre distinctions must be absolute, and it ignores the fact that the best writers for children frequently bend these distinctions. The final chapters of Pullman's *The Amber Spyglass* (2000), for example, blend fantasy with the Young Adult Novel. If one defines "postmodernism" as an agglomeration of different styles, then perhaps the way to understand the *Harry Potter* books is through the ways that they take on aspects of fantasy, the Young Adult Novel, fairy tales, the boarding school novel, the Bildungsroman, and all the many genres that Rowling's creative gifts have transformed into something new. The *Harry Potter* novels invite multiple readings for all the layers of meaning they contain, and the game of uncovering these meanings continues long after our first reading. Should the eclecticism of her innovative synthesis cause some meanings to go over the heads of her young readers, Rowling is not worried. "If they love them enough," she says, "they'll reread them. And then it will be like finding another sweet in the bag" (Mehren).

3

Reviews of the Novels

Initial reviews in both Great Britain and the United States were generally favorable. One of the first reviews (and perhaps *the* first) appeared in *The Scotsman* on June 28, 1997. In it, Lindsey Fraser wrote, "Rowling uses classic narrative devices with flair and originality and delivers a complex and demanding plot in the form of a hugely entertaining thriller. She is a first-rate writer for children." The following month, Scholastic paid more than $100,000 to publish the novel in the United States, and newspapers began to run "rags-to-riches" versions of Rowling's life story as well as more reviews of *Harry Potter and the Philosopher's Stone*. The *Sunday Telegraph* noted that while "Rowling-the-single-mother-in-a-garret is good hype material," this "should not detract from the fact that this is a terrific book," adding that the novel's "perfect blend of fantasy and down-to-earth characters" makes it an "ideal antidote to a glut of grim social-realist fiction for eight- to twelve-year-olds" (Hall). *The Times* (of London) called Rowling "a sparkling new author brimming with delicious ideas, glorious characters and witty dialogue," and the *Financial Times* declared her "an exciting new talent" whose "writing is endlessly imaginative and funny" (Johnson; Hopkinson). By the time the first novel was published as *Harry Potter and the Sorcerer's Stone* in the United States, Rowling's first two Harry Potter novels had already topped adult hardback best-seller lists in Great Britain, and news of her success began to appear in America. As in Great Britain, reviewers liked Harry. In September 1998, The *Columbus Dispatch*'s Nancy Gilson wrote, in one of the earliest American reviews of the novel, "The plot rolls smoothly, with action and invention as swift and surprising as sparks from a wand." Two months later, the *Boston Globe* thought the last few pages felt "rushed and second-rate" but, on the whole, deemed it "a charming, imaginative, magical confection of a novel" (Rosenberg). *Newseek*'s Carla Power and *The Christian Science Monitor*'s Yvonne Zipp went further still, the former rehearsing "Rowling's Cinderella-like story" before ranking the book alongside classic fantasies by C. S. Lewis and Roald Dahl and the latter comparing it to Dahl's *Charlie and the Chocolate Factory* and L. Frank Baum's *The Wizard of Oz*. In the *New York Times Book Review*, Michael Winerip found the first Harry Potter novel to be "funny, moving and impressive," and he suggested that Rowling, like Harry, "has soared beyond her modest Muggle surroundings to achieve something quite special."

When Winerip's review appeared in February of 1999, Rowling had already become a celebrity in Great Britain and was on the brink of becoming one in the United States. As a consequence, in reviews of the next three books in the series, some reviewers responded to the books themselves—but others did not distinguish the books from the phenomenon surrounding them. At first, swept up in the enthusiasm, those who conflated the *Harry Potter* novels with the Harry Potter phenomenon tended to produce enthusiastic reviews. When *Harry Potter and the Chamber of Secrets* was published (July 1998 in Great Britain, May 1999 in America), most reviewers embraced the novels. In Great Britain, *Chamber of Secrets* was hailed as being "as compulsive as the last" by *The Herald*, deemed "just as unputdownable" by the *Sunday Telegraph*, thought "better" than the first by the *Daily Telegraph*, and to have "everything a good sequel should have—the same formula as the original but with extra action and more jokes" by *The Independent*

(Johnstone; Hall; Bradman; Phelan). The first U.S. reviews echoed those from Great Britain, but later reviews grew more skeptical. *USA Today* and the *St. Louis Post-Dispatch* both praised the series, the latter calling Harry "a classic orphan who—I will bet—can hold his own with Little Orphan Annie and Oliver Twist" (Sawyer). The *Christian Science Monitor's* Zipp again placed the Harry Potter novels among the classics: "A new book by J. K. Rowling is almost as much cause for rejoicing as the discovery of an eighth Narnia manuscript tucked away in the wardrobe." The aforementioned reviews were all published by the end of June 1999, the month that the Harry Potter novels became a full-blown phenomenon in America as well as Great Britain.

Harry Potter and the Chamber of Secrets entered the *New York Times* hardcover bestseller list at number one on June 20, 1999, and on June 21, Rowling appeared on the *Rosie O'Donnell Show*. O'Donnell introduced Rowling as the "author of a book I could not put down—two books, actually" and exhorted viewers to "buy them both." The studio audience responded with polite, vigorous clapping as Rowling walked on stage; later, however, when Rowling mentioned that Warner Bros. had bought the movie rights, the crowd erupted in spontaneous applause. Either the growing popular appeal of the series was beginning to make some critics more skeptical, or the hype beginning to surround the books was raising expectations. In a *Washington Post* review published in July, Michael Dirda thought *Chamber of Secrets* "seems slightly less magical than the original if only because we've been here before." Similarly, *Horn Book's* Martha V. Parravano admitted that "the story whizzes along" but thought the book "feels a tad [. . .] formulaic" (472–473). That same month, the *Boston Globe's* Liz Rosenberg found the novel "as unput-downable" as its predecessor but believed that the *Harry Potter* books lack "the underlying meaning of the Narnia books" and "the dreamlike, satirical planned non-sense of Lewis Carroll." Nonetheless, she felt that "Rowling's genius stands far above the average series writer today" and that future books would resonate more deeply.

By the time *Prisoner of Azkaban* was published (July 1999 in Great Britain, September 1999 in America), most opinions of *Harry Potter* fell into one of four categories: (1) praise for the books, because they either entice children to read or prove that children's literature is worthy of adult attention; (2) scorn directed at people in the first group and, by extension, at the Harry Potter phenomenon, for a variety of reasons; (3) conservative U.S. Christians suggesting that the books should be removed from school libraries; and (4) the debate over whether the novels deserved to be ranked with classic children's fiction. To begin with the first group, many librarians have credited the series with encouraging children to read, and their remarks—or similar ones—frequently appear in news reports from this period. In *The Wall Street Journal*, Danielle Crittenden even enlisted the books against an imagined "anti-boy lobby," suggesting that because Harry Potter speaks to "the true nature of boys," the series would not only inspire boys to read but help them "to grow up into brave and even heroic men." The books have drawn readers of both genders, however, and their popularity soon drew the ire of those who harbor suspicions against all things popular. First in Great Britain and then in America, some critics began attacking the phenomenon using the books as a target. Writing in *The Independent* (London), children's author Terence Blacker criticized "Gurgling, sentimental editorials" on Harry Potter and claimed that the title character provides the "perfect hero for the 1990s," because the protagonist's story provides a "nannyish moral certainty" and supports "Blairite social conservatism with a smiling liberal face." Comparing Harry Potter fans to "heroin addicts [. . .] growing old in tandem with a fictional character," *Scotland on Sunday*'s Alan Taylor asserted that "Harry Potter's universe is morally bland and simple," and he felt that the books themselves were hardly classics: "As a stylist, she is competent rather than inspired. Her sentences do not sing, there is no music in her prose." Though Pico Iyer does not seem to share Taylor's or Blacker's scorn for the novels, his essay in the *New York Times Book Review* did develop many parallels between Rowling's fiction and contemporary Great Britain. After a favorable comparison between the *Harry Potter* novels and children's classics, he wrote: "What makes the Harry Potter books fly, so to speak, is not so much their otherwordliness as their fidelity to the way things really are (or were, at least, when quills and parchment were still more common than computers): wizards, Harry Potter's world suggests, are only regular muggles who've been to the right school."

Whether the books should be in schools at all became a topic of debate in America during the latter half of 1999. Prompted by *Time* magazine's September cover story on Harry Potter, which excerpted Lupin's description of the Dementors and included Rowling's promise that "there will be deaths" in future novels, parents in South Carolina, Georgia, Minnesota, Michigan, New York, Colorado, and California accused the books of being anti-Christian, of promoting witchcraft, and of exerting a morally dangerous influence on children. As Elizabeth Mounce of Columbia, South Carolina, said in a comment reproduced in many British and American papers, "The books have a serious tone of death, hate, lack of respect, and sheer evil" (Galloway). Despite the efforts of Muggles for Harry Potter (http://www.mugglesforharrypotter.org) and others, Harry's opponents succeeded in placing Rowling's Harry Potter novels at the top the American Library Association's list of the Most Challenged Books of 1999. Judy Blume, whose books frequently appear on this list, mocked the book-banners in an October 1999 op-ed piece in the *New York Times:* "At the rate we're going, I can imagine next year's headline: '*Goodnight Moon* Banned for Encouraging Children to Communicate with Furniture.'" The parody newspaper *The Onion* went a step further, satirizing conservative Christians in an article jokingly titled "*Harry Potter* Books Spark Rise in Satanism Among Children." For her part, Rowling has said "kill[ing] someone the reader cares about" demonstrates how evil Voldemort is, and that "If you ban all books with witchcraft and the supernatural, you'll ban three-quarters of children's literature" (Gray; Weeks). If people find the books objectionable, she has a "very basic solution: Don't read them" (Weeks). Of course, not all conservative Christians advocated banning the *Harry Potter* series. In her May–June 2000 *Horn Book* article, Kimbra Wilder Gish, a self-identified conservative Christian, carefully outlined the Biblical bases of potential objections to the *Harry Potter* novels. However, she suggested that if a child of ardent Christians "has a strong interest in these books, parents can use them as a learning experience," teaching the child "how to be a thoughtful reader, recognizing what good things one might take from these books as well as the things best left behind" (270).

Whether history would leave the *Harry Potter* books behind once the phenomenon subsides emerged more frequently in reviews of *Harry Potter and the Prisoner of Azkaban*. Comparing the *Harry Potter* books to classic novels raises the standards by which most books are reviewed, and it reflects the feeling that Rowling's work must justify its popularity by competing with that of Carroll, Lewis, Dahl, or Baum. Glasgow's *Herald* praised *Azkaban* as "easily the best book of the series so far," but it also cautioned that the series was strictly for children: "These are not strictly timeless stories" but "Enid Blyton with broomsticks" (Judah). Writing in the *New Statesman*, Amanda Craig considered Rowling not "in Philip Pullman's league" but, rather, between Edith Nesbit and Roald Dahl, albeit "less subversive than either." That said, Craig praised Rowling's "capacity to both create and transmit joy," and she found the novel every bit as good as its two predecessors. Finding great depth in the novel, *The Guardian*'s strong review praised the book's darkness and moral complexity, noting that Harry must try "to make sense of surviving in a world where evil may adopt unexpected forms" (Lockerbie). *The Times*, *The Sunday Times*, and *The Irish Times* all deemed *Azkaban* to be Rowling's best work to date, the latter adding that "the pre-publication hype has been justified. This is, simply, a wizard book" (Dunbar). In the United States, most reviewers liked the third *Harry Potter* novel, albeit in varying degrees. Gregory Macguire, writing for the *New York Times Book Review*, felt that "in terms of plot, the books do nothing very new, but they do it brilliantly," while *USA Today*'s Cathy Hainer thought that Rowling had "score[d] another home run" with *Azkaban*. The *Boston Globe*'s Rosenberg said that Rowling "rises in many ways to new heights in this volume." However, taking exception with both the positive reviews and the phenomenon itself, the *Horn Book*'s Roger Sutton called the *Harry Potter* novels a "likeable but critically insignificant series" (500).

Prior to and following the publication of *Harry Potter and the Goblet of Fire* (on July 8, 2000, in both America and Great Britain), several critics felt compelled to announce just how insignificant the *Harry Potter* books were. The analyses by Philip Hensher, William Safire, and Harold Bloom are notable primarily for their snobbery, either toward children's literature as a genre or toward Harry Potter in particular for being so darn popular. Hensher's argument that the books lacked "literary merit" and would not become "classics" was undercut by his prejudices against literature for children, which were revealed when, anxious that *Harry Potter and the Prisoner of Azkaban* might win the Whitbread Prize instead of Seamus Heaney's translation of *Beowulf*, he announced, "What we ought to worry about is the infantilisation of adult culture, the loss of a sense of what a classic really is."[9] Two days after Hensher's piece appeared, Safire, thrilled that Rowling had not won the Whitbread Prize, praised the judges for awarding *Azkaban* "the lesser award [. . .] for best children's book," quoted Hensher on adult culture's decline, and revealed his own ignorance about children's literature and culture. Faulting the *Harry Potter* series for lacking depth, he held up L. Frank Baum's *The Wonderful Wizard of Oz* (1900) as a classic children's book, mentioning Dorothy's "transforming ruby red slippers"—and forgetting that they are red in the film but silver in the book. Having read only the first book in the *Harry Potter* series, Safire decided that the third was not "prizeworthy culture" but, rather, "a waste of adult time." Also believing that he need read no further than the first novel before making his critical pronouncement, Yale Professor Harold Bloom displayed more arrogance than acumen — rather disappointing, given that he is so widely read. He classified the book as "not well written," and he doubted it would "prove a classic of children's literature" because it lacks "an authentic imaginative vision." Though he did not reveal how one measures a work for the authenticity of its vision, he wrote, "Her prose style, heavy on cliché, makes no demands on its readers," thereby restricting his own analysis to New Critical clichés. In a condescending tone reminiscent of Draco Malfoy, Bloom asked, "Why read it? Presumably, if you cannot be persuaded to read anything better, Rowling will have to do." University of Minnesota Professor Jack Zipes, a scholar of children's literature, did not condescend in the manner of Bloom, Safire, or Hensher, but his analysis appears to rest upon the popularity of the books. "For anything to become a phenomenon in western society," he wrote, "it must become conventional." Rowling's novels "sell extraordinarily well precisely because they are so cute and ordinary." For Zipes, then, the success of the *Harry Potter* novels can only mean that they are ordinary and, by implication, unworthy of success.

The novels had sold so extraordinarily well that by the time *Harry Potter and the Goblet of Fire* was published, it received more reviews than any of its predecessors. Indeed, a few days before *Goblet* was for sale, George Will praised the *Harry Potter* books from the editorial pages of *The Washington Post*. On the day of publication, *The Times* of London ran its review as the leading article on the front page, with a headline announcing, "First review: new Harry Potter 'a cracker'." "And is it good? You bet it is," wrote Sarah Johnson. "Once again, Rowling packs the pages with witty and imaginative ideas." Reviews for *Goblet of Fire* were decidedly mixed, however. While the *Sunday Herald*'s Ian Bruce called the novel "a well-wrought 636-page thriller very much in the spirit of its trio of prequels that should further satisfy Rowling's young readers," *The Observer's* Robert McCrum thought it "bulky but light," adding that Rowling's "work teems with exotic personnel and it has the reader by the throat from page to page, but her prose is as flat (and as English) as old beer." Janet Maslin of the *New York Times* expressed the belief that the novels would be considered classics by future readers and said that *Goblet of Fire* provided the "clearest proof yet of what should have been wonderfully obvious: what makes the Potter books so popular is the radically simple fact that they're so good." In contrast, *USA Today's* Dierdre Donahue wrote, "the fourth installment is a hurried novel that highlights Rowling's ability to crank out pages but shows less of her breathtaking creativity." Emblematic of the divided critical opinion, the *San Francisco Chronicle's* David Kipen called *Goblet of Fire* "a perfect teenager of a book. It's spotty. It's opinionated. It's often strangely endearing. Most of all, as widely reported, it's ungainly."

Indicative of Harry Potter's high profile, *Goblet* garnered reviews from Stephen King in the *New York Times Book Review*, Joan Acocella in the *New Yorker*, Tim Wynne-Jones in the *Ottawa Citizen*, Penelope Lively in *The Independent*, and Julia Briggs in the *Times Literary Supplement*. Briggs, the biographer of E. Nesbit, called the series "a transparent, yet entirely engaging piece of wish-fulfillment" and offered praise for "the comic inventions that are her forte—the owl service, the game of 'quidditch', the ghost in the loo, as well as a menagerie of monsters." In what might be termed faint praise, she said of Rowling, "well constructed and paced, her writing is often frightening, but seldom mysterious." Lively, winner of the 1987 Booker Prize, dismissed claims of the series being "derivative" ("Everything is derivative, looked at in one way. In critical circles, it is called intertextuality"), but felt that *Goblet* was "too long" and criticized the prepublication hype. King, the bestselling horror novelist, confessed that, while in the hospital recuperating from being struck by a car, the second and third *Harry Potter* novels "became a kind of lifeline for me." He liked the novels because they are "shrewd mystery tales," fun, and funny; *Goblet of Fire*, he wrote, "is every bit as good as Potters 1 through 3" (13). In her *New Yorker* article, Acocella admitted, "I would love to tell you that the book is a great big nothing. In fact, it's wonderful, just like its predecessors" (74). Citing "traditionalism" as the "secret of Rowling's success," Acocella explained, "Rowling's books are chock-a-block with archetypes, and she doesn't just use them; she glories in them, postmodernly" (74). In an otherwise positive review, children's author Wynne-Jones touched on a theme that troubled several reviewers: the depiction of "foreigners" in *Goblet*. Wynne-Jones observed, "The appearance of 'foreigners' give us reason to cavil with Rowling. Fleur is portrayed as snooty, the Durmstrang crowd as shifty and unctuous." That said, "The stereotyping isn't heinous so much as cliched, the stuff of comic books." If some found Rowling to be oversimplifying real-world issues, *The Irish Times'* Niall Macmonagle took the opposite position: "Rowling asks her readers to think serious thoughts about serious matters in Muggleland, including bullying, privacy, broken friendship, political self-advancement and, most movingly of all, the relationship between parent and child."

Many reviews of *Harry Potter and the Goblet of Fire* analyzed the entire series to this point, and several articles on Rowling's novels deserve mention. In addition to Acocella's *New Yorker* piece on the first four novels, Alison Lurie offered an appraisal of the first three, in which she viewed Harry's story "as a metaphor for the power of childhood: of imagination, of creativity, and of humor," expressing admiration for the "psychological subtlety" of Rowling's characters: even "the good characters are not perfect." However, if one measures critical commentary in terms of the frequency of insights per paragraph, Polly Shulman and A. O. Scott's epistolary discussion at the on-line magazine *Slate* ranks at the top of the thousands of articles published about Rowling. Though conducted in August 1999, their exchange even anticipated the conservative Christian backlash, which began to gather force the following month. Prefiguring Lurie's remarks on Rowling's characters, Shulman speculated that Rowling's "refusal to drum in lessons" helps to explain her vast readership: "her books get their depth from a combination of allegory and genuine human interactions that haven't been pre-chewed. She lets her characters learn from their mistakes (or fail to do so)." Comparing the *Harry Potter* series to serialized novels, she observed that it "has some of the excitement that Dickens' readers must have felt as they read his novels in serial form, knowing he was working frantically on the next installment." Both noted the "young adult" themes of the novels, and Scott offered the intriguing analogy between being a wizard and being gay: "You grow up in a hostile world governed by codes and norms that seem nonsensical to you, and you discover at a certain age that there are people like you—what's more there's a whole subculture with its own codes and norms right alongside the straight (muggle) one, yet strangely invisible to it." It would be hard to top the richness of their analyses, so it should not be surprising that the letters of Jodi Kantor and Judith Shulevitz, published at *Slate* in July 2000, do not quite measure up to Shulman and Scott's. Nonetheless, Shulevitz's comments on house-elves (a subplot of *Goblet* that troubled several reviewers) and comparison between Voldemort and *King Lear*'s Edmund are worth noting. Voldemort, like Edmund, wishes to "punish the world" for having his "social status determined by [his] parents' marital relations, or lack thereof." Finally, a thorough if contradictory examination of the first three *Harry Potter* novels, Nicholas Tucker's "The Rise and Rise of Harry Potter," embodies the range of opinions on the books: the first half of the article disparages the series, and the second half finds reasons for praise. Throughout, however, Tucker grounds his commentary in a thorough knowledge of Rowling's literary antecedents.

4

The Performance of the Novels

Though the *Harry Potter* series bears the influences of many earlier works of literature, the speed and scope of its success are quite new. While Dr. Seuss's *Oh! The Places You'll Go* (1990), Richard Adams's *Watership Down* (1972), and E. B. White's *Charlotte's Web* (1952) have all made their mark on "adult" bestseller lists, the *Harry Potter* novels are the first books for children to achieve such an incredible level of popular success. Within a few months of its publication, *Harry Potter and the Philosopher's Stone* had landed on the British hardback bestseller charts and the next three volumes went straight to the top of these charts upon their release. In the late twentieth and early twenty-first century, J. K. Rowling became one of the most widely read authors in the English-speaking world.

On the grounds that children's literature should be excluded from an *adult* bestseller list, some lists have not included the novels. The *Sunday Times'* bestseller charts refused to document the novels because, as literary editor Caroline Gascoigne explained, "We have never included children's books on our main bestseller list, it's as simple as that. We have our reputation as the most prestigious and reliable list to think of. That is why Harry is on the children's bestseller list instead" (Gibbons). Despite this strict prohibition, the *Sunday Times* did include literature such as the novelization of *Star Wars, Episode I: The Phantom Menace*. The *New York Times Book Review*'s treatment of the *Harry Potter* books is, perhaps, even more telling of cultural prejudices against children's literature. At first, the *Book Review* permitted the novels to remain on the list, but as they rose to the top spots, Scholastic's rivals began asking if the *Harry Potter* novels might be removed, because their domination prevented other (adult) books from receiving the *New York Times* bestseller imprimatur. On July 23, 2000, the day that *Harry Potter and the Goblet of Fire* would have given Rowling four of top five spots on the list, the Potter novels suddenly disappeared from it—re-emerging on a "Children's Best Sellers" list. *Book Review* editor Charles McGrath admitted that "Harry Potter was the catalyst" for changing the *Book Review*'s list. "It's a phenomenon that will not go away," he said ("Turning a page at the Book Review"). As long as McGrath remains editor, subdividing the *Book Review*'s list is also a phenomenon that seems unlikely to go away: on September 10, 2000, he rearranged the children's list into "Paperback," "Picture," and "Chapter" lists, one of which has been printed in the *Book Review* each week since then. Predictably, Scholastic was not pleased at the fact that its *Harry Potter* books no longer appear every week.

Before earning the distinction of shattering the *New York Times* bestseller lists into increasingly specialized fragments, Harry Potter tested the limits of international copyright laws. Bloomsbury published the first novel in the summer of 1997, but Scholastic did not publish it until the fall of 1998. Although Scholastic did not plan to publish the second novel until September 1999, Bloomsbury had already published it in July 1998. By early April 1999, so many eager American readers had bought the Bloomsbury edition from Amazon.com's British website that Scholastic objected, claiming the online bookseller had violated the U.S. publisher's territorial rights. In response, Amazon.co.uk limited purchases by U.S. customers to one copy per order, and Scholastic printed *Harry Potter and the Chamber of Secrets* in May 1999, four months ahead of schedule. The problem briefly recurred when Bloomsbury published *Harry Potter and the Prisoner of Azkaban* in July 1999, and Scholastic, again ahead of its schedule, published the novel in September. To avoid future transAtlantic copyright disputes, *Harry Potter and the Goblet of Fire* was published in both the United States and Great Britain on the same day in July 2000, the two Harry Potter school books were published on the same day in March 2001, and Bloomsbury and Scholastic have agreed to publish all future *Harry Potter* novels simultaneously.

Though word of mouth played a significant role in the first book's sales on each side of the Atlantic, all of the *Harry Potter* novels soon benefited from the publishers' marketing campaigns and from the media hype surrounding the series. Prior to the British release of the third novel, Bloomsbury adopted what *The Times* of London called "a Disney-style 'teaser' technique," placing empty Harry Potter display bins in stores, "tantalizingly promising that *Harry Potter and the Prisoner of Azkaban* is coming soon" (Johnson, "Just Wild about Harry"). When the books went on sale in Great Britain in July 1999, not all schools were closed for vacation, and bookshops therefore refused to sell it until 3:45 PM so that children would not skip school to buy it. The fourth novel, which was released at midnight on July 8, 2000, prompted booksellers to host Harry Potter parties, with parents and children staying up very late to get *Goblet of Fire*. Further increasing the suspense, the publishers refused to divulge even the title of the novel. Plain white boxes shipped to bookstores read "Harry Potter IV. National Street/On-Sale Date July 8, 2000. Not To Be Sold Before July 8, 2000." That said, one young reader in Virginia found a copy for sale a week before the official release, and the book's title did make it to the press. Each Christmas season, both Bloomsbury and Scholastic have marketed boxed sets of all the novels published to date, and both publishers sell fancier editions at a higher price. Bloomsbury has also published "special editions" of the first three novels, and Scholastic is selling a deluxe edition of *Sorcerer's Stone*, charging $75 for gilt-edged pages and an original illustration of Harry drawn by Rowling herself. As early as October 1998, Bloomsbury, recognizing Harry Potter's crossover appeal, was selling two paperback editions of *Philosopher's Stone*, one with a cover marketed to children, and one with a cover marketed to adults. As each installment of the series has been released in paperback, Bloomsbury has continued offering two editions so that adults may, without fear of embarrassment, read Rowling's books as they ride to work on the train. Even Bloomsbury's audio books, unabridged and read by Stephen Fry, come with different covers, the "adult" version being a bit more expensive than the "child" version. Scholastic, which has not created separate adult and child covers, has produced unabridged audio books performed by Jim Dale. The differences between the American and British audio books are that Fry pronounces the "t" in "Voldemort" but Dale pronounces the word with a French accent (no "t"). Dale also speaks in a British accent that is less strong than Fry's, presumably to reduce the risk of American listeners mis-hearing him.

The main difference between the Bloomsbury and Scholastic audio books is the text itself. Assisted by Rowling, Scholastic's Arthur A. Levine has translated each of the novels from British English into American English, an act that has received its share of criticism. When the fourth novel, *Harry Potter and the Goblet of Fire*, was published, Peter H. Gleick's op-ed piece in the *New York Times* lamented the "devolution from English to 'American' English" and suggested that Scholastic's "Americanized" texts contribute to the "dumb[ing] down" of U.S. society. In the previous year, responding to a brief report on the topic in the *New Yorker*, then-eleven-year old Whitaker E. Cohen criticized Levine, asserting that children "have large imaginations, and can usually figure out [. . .] what words mean from their context." For his part, Levine has said, "I wasn't trying to, quote, 'Americanize' them. What I was trying to do was translate, which is something different. I wanted to make sure that an American kid reading the book would have the same literary experience that a British kid would have" (Radosh). In Levine's defense, the books are a highly public example of a common editorial practice, and indeed, many works for children undergo much more radical transformations than the *Harry Potter* novels have. That said, however, one might wonder about Levine's assumption that it is not only possible but desirable to create "the same literary experience" for children from different countries. The first three books received the greatest degree of translation, and *Harry Potter and the Philosopher's Stone* underwent the most changes. In addition to removing from its American title the reference to alchemy, Levine and Rowling changed "jumper" to "sweater," "football" to "soccer," "Quidditch pitch" to "Quidditch field," "crumpets" to "English muffins," "mum" to "mom" (though "mum" was retained in later books), and "sherbet lemon" to "lemon drop," to name a few examples. Perhaps because the manuscript reached Scholastic's offices too late for extensive translation or because of a change in editorial policy, *Harry Potter and the Goblet of Fire* remains quite unchanged in its American edition. Not only is (for instance) "sherbet lemon" retained, but Scholastic's *Literature Guide* for *Goblet* even acknowledges differences between British and American English: a worksheet titled "Learning English" explains, "Harry and his friends speak English, but they don't always use the same words Americans do," and it provides two lists of words, inviting American readers to "Match each word Harry uses to the one(s) you would say" (Beech 22).

Foreign-language translations have been published in Brazil, Bulgaria, China, Croatia, the Czech Republic, Denmark, Estonia, Finland, France, Germany, Greece, Hungary, Iceland, Indonesia, Israel,

Italy, Japan, Korea, The Netherlands, Norway, Poland, Portugal, Romania, Spain, and Sweden. While the Chinese read about Ha-li Bote (Harry Potter), the Italians meet il Professore Silencio (Dumbledore), and the French learn to dislike le Professeur Rogue (Snape), Harry Potter's influence on the English language can be seen in British and American editorials, political cartoons, and even everyday expressions. In *The Independent*, a review of *Captive State: The Corporate Takeover of Britain* began by calling George Monbiot, the book's author, "the Harry Potter of British public life" because, "Bespectacled, slightly disheveled and boyishly endearing, he gives the impression of being earnestly engaged in the great battle between good and evil. In his case, Voldemort is what used to be called Big Business" (Aaronovitch). In contrast, the American publication *Entrepreneur* was quick to claim the series as pro-capitalist, claiming that "behind the magic and the mystery hides an entrepreneurial tale" (Williams). Likewise, many newspaper articles with no ostensible connection to the *Harry Potter* series have drawn upon the novels for their metaphors. *New York Times* op-ed columnist Gail Collins, an unabashed fan of *Harry Potter*, wrote in April 2000 that "Mrs. Clinton as a candidate is Hermione Granger. She wants to sign up for all the courses, and if there's a scheduling conflict, she'll replicate" ("Rudy's identity crisis"). On a day when Collins's column began with a reference to Harry Potter ("An ode to July"), Thomas L. Friedman's op-ed piece on the Palestinian-Israeli peace process bore the title "Lebanon and the Goblet of Fire." Affirming Rowling's hold on the op-ed page, in an October 2000 column, Maureen Dowd wrote, "On the whole, the president has been patient about Al Gore casting him as Lord Voldemort, the Harry Potter villain who inspires such fear that no one dares speak his name."

In addition to appearing in Lynn Johnston's "For Better or for Worse," Dean Young and Denis Lebrun's "Blondie," Jeff and Bil Keane's "Family Circus," Bob Browne's "Hi and Lois," Darby Conley's "Get Fuzzy," and one of Charles Schulz's last "Peanuts" strips, Harry starred in cartoons about the 2000 American presidential election, reality-based TV, and computers. *The Oregonian's* Jack Ohman drew Al Gore choosing Harry as his running mate, the *Louisville Courier-Journal's* Nick Anderson showed a child reading *Harry Potter* while his parents watched "Reality T.V.," and Marshall Ramsey of the *Clarion Ledger* (of Jackson, Mississippi) depicted a child reading *Harry Potter* while his computer languished unused.[10] The *Wall Street Journal* devoted a front-page story to the Harry's hold on the popular imagination, noting that *Newsday* "called sprinter Michael Johnson a 'muggle' for flaming out of the Olympic 200-meter trials" and that the Chicago *Daily Herald* compared an NBC Olympics commentator to Dementors, presumably because he "suck[ed] the joy out of people" (Rose and Nelson A1). *Sports Illustrated* even imagined a memo from the National Collegiate Athletic Association (NCAA) to Dumbledore, accusing him of "potentially serious rules infractions within [his] Quidditch program," including bending the rules to let Harry play during his first year at Hogwarts and allowing Lucius Malfoy's gift of "state-of-the-art broomsticks" to buy a place for Draco on the Slytherin team ("What if Quidditch"). As the *Wall Street Journal* article contended, "Potterisms are moving into the everyday language of work, politics and romance, where they are offering the series' millions of fans a new insiders' short hand for all manner of good and evil" (A1).

In a July 2000 cartoon that anticipated the marketing of Harry Potter products by a few months, Dan Wasserman drew two children, one carrying a *Harry Potter* book as they walk down a street past shops selling Happy Harry Meals, Wizard Fries, Muggle Mugs, and "Harry Schlock." One child says to the other, "I can already see how it ends—the dark forces win." Warner Bros., which is producing films of the books, has licensed a range of products: Lego toys, a card game, a board game, puzzles, address books, calendars, journals, stickers, T-shirts, sweatshirts, mugs, trading cards, figurines,

Bertie Bott's Every Flavour Beans, a Nimbus 2000 broomstick that emits "flying sounds," an electronic dragon named "Roarin' Snorin' Norbert," an activity kit called "Professor Sprout's Fungus Field Trip," and far more than can be listed here (Barnes). The first film, to be titled *Harry Potter and the Philosopher's Stone* in Great Britain and *Harry Potter and the Sorcerer's Stone* in the United States, is scheduled to be released on November 16, 2001. Directed by Chris Columbus, who is best known for the films *Mrs. Doubtfire* and *Home Alone*, the movie stars eleven-year-old Daniel Radcliffe in the title role, with ten-year-old Emma Watson and twelve-year-old Rupert Grint as Harry's friends, Hermione Granger and Ron Weasley. Grint and Watson are newcomers, but Radcliffe played young David in the BBC's *David Copperfield*, and the supporting cast features many familiar names: Robbie Coltrane as Hagrid, Richard Harris as Albus Dumbledore, Alan Rickman as Severus Snape, Dame Maggie Smith as Minerva McGonagall, Julie Walters as Mrs. Weasley, Fiona Shaw as Aunt Petunia, and John Cleese as Nearly Headless Nick. Rowling's response to both film and its attendant marketing, however, has been decidedly ambivalent. She has said she is looking forward to seeing Quidditch on the big screen, and she thinks the right actors have been cast for the parts. Yet, prior to the production of the Harry Potter toys, she remarked, "I can only say now to all the parents out there that if the action figures are horrible, just tell the kids: don't buy them! Sorry, Warner's" (Stahl). In response to Rowling's concern that action figures may promote violent play, Mattel has agreed to call its figures "collectible characters" (Barnes).

Though movies and Harry Potter toys will add to Rowling's financial well-being, the novels themselves have already made her one of the wealthiest women in Great Britain. In 1999, London's *The Mirror* placed Rowling third on a list of Britain's wealthiest women, ahead of the Spice Girls (who ranked jointly at number six), supermodel Kate Moss (number eighteen), and *Bridget Jones* author

Helen Fielding (number forty-one). In 2000, Rowling topped the list. Harry has brought considerable financial rewards to his publishers, too. Bloomsbury Publishing's *1998 Annual Report* says that 763,000 copies of the first two Harry Potter books had been sold (9). Though it offers no total number of books sold for the entire series, *1999 Annual Report* discloses sales of 1.3 million paperbacks (of the first two novels) and 1.25 million copies for *Harry Potter and the Prisoner of Azkaban*. It also reports, "The increase in backlist revenues and the economics of scale derived from the large print runs on the Harry Potter series increased gross profit margins by 1.6% to 51.7% (1998, 50.1%)" (7). In 2000, Bloomsbury's edition of *Harry Potter and the Goblet of Fire* sold 5.3 million copies before it had even been published. Scholastic's sales have been comparably robust. By December 1998, *Harry Potter and the Sorcerer's Stone* was approaching 100,000 copies in print and was going back to press for a third time ("U.K.'s number one best-seller"). In 2000, Scholastic did an initial print run of 3.8 million copies of *Harry Potter and the Goblet of Fire*, which sold nearly three million copies in its first week, becoming one of the fastest-selling books ever (Mutter and Milliot). Including all editions (hardback and paperback), Scholastic reported 45.3 million copies of the Harry Potter books in print as of late November 2000 ("Scholastic joins"); by early March 2001, forty-nine million copies were in print (Barnes). Published in the same month, the two Harry Potter school books had a combined first printing of ten million copies, five million by Scholastic and five million by Bloomsbury (Holt).

The popular appeal of the series is matched by the many awards it has received. In 1997, *Harry Potter and the Philosopher's Stone* won the Gold Medal in the Nestlé Smarties Book Prize, was the Overall winner and won the Longer Novel Category in the FCBG Children's Book Awards, and was declared Children's Book of the Year by the British Book Awards. It also won the Birmingham Cable Children's Book Award in 1997, and both the Young Telegraph Paperback of the Year and the Sheffield Children's Book Award in 1998. Jim Dale's recording of *Harry Potter and the Sorcerer's Stone* was nominated for a Grammy Award, and the book won an ABBY from American Booksellers. In 1998, *Harry Potter and the Chamber of Secrets* again won the Nestlé Smarties Book Prize, the same two FCBG Children's Book Awards, and was named Children's Book of the Year by the British Book Awards. It also won the Scottish Arts Council Children's Book Award, the North East Scotland Book Award, and Rowling was named the Bookseller Author of the Year by the Booksellers Association. By late 1999, *Harry Potter and the Prisoner of Azkaban* and Seamus Heaney's translation of *Beowulf* had both been nominated for the Whitbread Prize, which generated such ridiculous headlines as HARRY POTTER V. BEOWULF IN LITERARY COMBAT (Prynn). When the awards were announced in January of 2000, *Beowulf* won the main award, and *Azkaban* won the Whitbread's Children's Book of the Year. In 1999, *Azkaban* also won the Nestlé Smarties Book Prize, the FCBG Children's Book Award, and Rowling was named Author of the Year by both the Booksellers Association and the British Book Awards. In 2001, Jim Dale's audio book of *Harry Potter and the Goblet of Fire* won a Grammy Award.

5

Further Reading
and Discussion Questions

Rowling's only other published works are the two Harry Potter school books: *Fantastic Beasts and Where to Find Them* by Newt Scamander, and *Quidditch Through the Ages* by Kennilworthy Whisp. Both published in March 2001, these are delightful genre parodies but fairly quick reads. So, while awaiting the fifth novel, fans of Rowling should enjoy the works of Philip Pullman, David Almond, and Diana Wynne Jones. Pullman's *His Dark Materials* trilogy—*Northern Lights* (1995, retitled *The Golden Compass* in the United States), *The Subtle Knife* (1997), and *The Amber Spyglass* (2000)—may be of a slightly higher reading level than the *Harry Potter* novels, but it is just as good, and many reviewers consider it to be better. Though its narrative is just as driven by character as Rowling's, Pullman's series is certainly darker, more philosophical, and more willing to probe thorny theological issues. Rowling's series may be closest in spirit to Diana Wynne Jones's *Chrestomanci* quartet: *Charmed Life* (1977), *The Magicians of Caprona* (1980), *Witch Week* (1982), and *The Lives of Christopher Chant* (1988). Linked by the character of Chrestomanci, the novels are otherwise independent and can be read in any order. Consider beginning with the final two books, which in addition to being the best written of the series combine school settings with magic. See also Jones's *Year of the Griffin* (2000), about a wizards' university in financial straits and the sequel to *Dark Lord of Derkholm* (1998), as well as *The Tough Guide to Fantasyland* (1996), a guidebook parody that anticipates the Harry Potter school books. In *Skellig* (1998), *Kit's Wilderness* (1999), and *Heaven's Eyes* (2000), David Almond deftly blends fantasy with social realism and "young adult" themes. Though Rowling's work addresses "real" issues in a fantastic setting, Almond's novels are closer to magical realism: they are set in a "real" world woven through with dreams, myths, and the spiritual.

The *Harry Potter* novels might also serve as an introduction to classic fantasy series like J. R. R. Tolkien's *Lord of the Rings* (and especially its precursor, *The Hobbit*), Ursula K. Le Guin's four Earthsea novels, Susan Cooper's *Dark Is Rising* quintet, Lloyd Alexander's chronicles of Pyrdain, C. S. Lewis's seven Narnia books, and E. Nesbit's trilogy about Cyril, Robert, Anthea, and Jane. Those who think the gender roles in Rowling's novels are regressive may be further disappointed by Susan Cooper's characters, despite the well-plotted and suspenseful middle three books: *The Dark Is Rising* (1973), *Greenwitch* (1974), and the *High King* (1975). As particular favorites of Rowling, Lewis's Narnia septet and E. Nesbit's trilogy—*The Five Children and It* (1902), *The Phoenix and the Carpet* (1904), and *The Story of the Amulet* (1906)—might be the novels with which to begin exploring fantasy. A work that Rowling often mentions as her favorite book from childhood, Elizabeth Goudge's *The Little White Horse*, combines sharp observation of social behaviors with mystical fantasy in a nineteenth-century Cornwall setting. Though Goudge's novel clearly bears the influence of Austen, to appreciate the degree to which Jane influenced Joanne, *Pride and Prejudice* (1813) and the gothic parody *Northanger Abbey* (1818) make excellent introductions to her work. More vicious in his satire than Austen, Roald Dahl delights in exposing the hypocrisy of "normal" people, an outlook clearly shared by Rowling. The first sentence of *Harry Potter and the Philosopher's Stone* would be at home in almost any of Dahl's novels for children. Though some adults find Dahl's work too cruel and unsuitable for younger readers, children have enjoyed the unsympathetic view of witches in *The Witches* (1983) and the spirited lampooning of nasty adults in *Matilda* (1988) and other works. In her tone, wit, and satire, Eva Ibbotson suggests a gentler Dahl, and those who enjoy Rowling's sense of humor should read Ibbotson's *Which Witch?* (1979) and *The Secret of Platform 13* (1994).

In addition to the websites listed below, the best secondary sources on Harry Potter are Elizabeth D. Schafer's *Exploring Harry Potter* (2000), Lindsey Fraser's *Telling Tales: An Interview with J. K. Rowling* (2000), and Linda Ward Beech's *Scholastic Literature Guides* (2000) to each of the novels. Schafer's book, a volume in *Beacham's Sourcebooks for Teaching Young Adult Fiction,* will be of most interest to teachers, but scholars, general readers, and students may enjoy it, too. A reference work, *Exploring Harry Potter* offers an overview of major themes, mythology, history, magic, and many topics related to the series, as well as connections both within and beyond the novels (including suggestions for further reading). Beech's paperback guides were designed for use by teachers and are geared toward teaching students in the United States. Fraser, who wrote one of the first published reviews of *Harry Potter and the Philosopher's Stone*, offers a valuable addition to Mammoth's *Telling Tales* series. The sixty-page paperback consists primarily of an interview with Rowling, but it also provides an overview of the first three books. Other great biographical resources are "The not especially fascinating life so far of J. K. Rowling" (http://www.okukbooks.com/harry/rowling.htm), an autobiographical essay that *was* at OKUK Books's website but lately has been inaccessible, and Evan Solomon's "J. K. Rowling interview" (http://cbc.ca/programs/sites/hottype_rowlingcomplete.html), which can still be found on the CBC's *Hot Type* website. Readers interested in imaginative interaction with the *Harry Potter* novels may want to take a look at (or even write some) fan fiction, some of which can be found the "Books" section of FanFiction.net (http://www.fanfiction.net).

Websites
Official Sites

Harry Potter Website (http://www.jkrowling.com/), owned by Christopher Little (Rowling's agent), lists all publishers of the Potter novels, links to them, and Mr. Little's contact information. *Harry Potter Books* (http://harrypotter.bloomsbury.com/harrypotter/), maintained by Bloomsbury (the British publisher of the Harry Potter novels), is really two websites. Clicking on "Witches and Wizards" leads to interactive website with information about who is involved in producing the books (editor, publicist, etc.), a biographical sketch of Rowling, the latest news, Frequently Asked Questions (FAQ), as well as invitations to join a fan club, send howlers and "owlers," or buy the books. Clicking on "Muggles" leads to the adults' site, which offers a biography, FAQ, news, awards, favorable reviews, an extensive glossary (of terms and names used in the novels), and allows the user to order the books. *Harry Potter* (http://www.scholastic.com/harrypotter/), run by Scholastic (Rowling's U.S. publisher), offers the most interactive "official site," including a chat room, two interviews, a challenging trivia game, an extensive pronunciation guide, and a "Discussion Guide for Teachers" by Kylene Beers, an Assistant Professor of Reading at the University of Houston, Texas. The site also sells Potter-related merchandise, though it does restrict itself to the more literary items:

books, journals, bookmarks, and stationery. As of February 2001, the Harry Potter movie website (http://harrypotter .warnerbros.com/), an elaborate graphics-driven site for Warner Bros.'s forthcoming film, offers the teaser, poster, news and events, press releases, photos, and a "Wizard's Shop." *Comic Relief: Harry's Books* (http://www.comi-crelief.com/harrysbooks/) provides information about Newt Sca-mander's *Fantastic Beasts and Where to Find Them* and Kennilwor-thy Whisp's *Quidditch Through the Ages*, the pseudonymously authored school books. The *Official Mary GrandPré Fan Club* (http://www.marygrandpre.org/) offers a biographical sketch of the illustrator of Scholastic's editions as well as her speaking schedule, FAQ, and artwork for sale. The *Jim Dale Home Page* (http://www.jim-dale.com/) provides a low-tech, but highly entertaining, visit with Jim Dale, who reads the U.S. audio books: he answers questions from readers, offers a bit of personal history, and reveals the real-life sources of some of the voices he has created.

Fan Sites

Though Warner Bros. claims that some of these Harry Potter pages violate the studio's intellectual property rights, fans have created hundreds of sites devoted to Harry. Those listed here are some of the best. The greatest features of Christie Chang's *Harry Potter Net-work* (http://www.hpnetwork.f2s.com/) are its "Spellbook" and its "Derivatives" page, explaining the origins of character names. An ambitious site, several sections remain "under construction," but in addition to the above-mentioned items, its list of miscellaneous facts, chat transcripts, and clean design all recommend it. Claire Field's *The Boy Who Lived* (http://www.harrypotterguide.co.uk/) is equal parts general reference work (several pages explaining terms, names, and places from the series), meta-reference work (as in its collection of covers from around the world), interactive site (see its survey, forum, and poll), and news (which, mercifully, it divides into "Book News," "Rumours," "General News," and "Movie News"). Warner Bros. requested that Ms. Field transfer the domain name, which she had registered, to them. Following an exchange of correspondence, this matter has now been resolved to the satisfaction of both parties. Jenna Robertson's *The Unofficial Harry Potter Fan Club* (http://www.geocities.com/harrypotterfans/), which has thus far avoided Warner Bros.'s legal scrutiny, may be the best fan site on Rowling. Its user-friendly design, cover gallery, news, book recommendations, and "Hedwig's Guide to Finding Harry Potter on the Web"—an extensive, annotated list of links—render Robertson's website an excellent resource. Indeed, readers interested in visiting the many sites not included here would do well to consult her links.

News Media

Some newspapers offer an archive of articles on Rowling, such as *Featured Author: J. K. Rowling* (http://www.nytimes.com/books/00/07/23/specials/rowling.html), maintained by the *New York Times*. Users have to register to use this site, but registration is free. Sites that do not require registration include *USA Today's Pottermania* (http://www.usatoday.com/life/enter/books/potter/index.htm) and include the now discontinued London *Times's Online Special: Harry Potter* (fortunately, searching the *Times*'s site still yields articles on Rowling). For those seeking satire, *Slate* offers "Harry Potter by all of the top editorial cartoonists" (http://cagle.slate.msn.com/news/harrypotter/main.asp). As the Web is always in flux, I maintain "J. K. Rowling on the Web" (http://www.ksu.edu/english/nelp/rowling/), a collection of links that I try to keep up to date.

Discussion Questions

1. Jonathan Levi said that *Harry Potter and the Goblet of Fire* was "the first children's book to endorse slavery since *Little Black Sambo.*" Do the Potter novels endorse the house-elves' enslavement? Consider the positions on elf-rights taken by Ron, George, Mr. Weasley, Dobby, Winky, Hermione, Sirius Black, and Harry. With whom are our sympathies supposed to lie?

2. If the *Harry Potter* novels endorse subjugation of the house-elves, do they endorse enslavement? Or should we instead see Rowling as recognizing the limitations of social reform? Are we supposed to be outraged at or sympathetic to George Weasley's statement that the house-elves are happy (*Goblet of Fire* 211)? A related point: Hermione says that the house-elves have been brainwashed into accepting their jobs. Should we agree with her? Do we see the means through which the elves are brainwashed?

3. As a corollary to the above two questions, consider the racial politics of the Harry Potter series. Angelina Johnson is black, Lee Jordan has dreadlocks, Cho Chang appears to be of Asian descent, and Parvati and Padma Patil have Indian-sounding names. Should anything be deduced from the elision of these characters' cultural backgrounds? Or are attitudes toward cultural differences expressed figuratively, through magical metaphors? That is, Voldemort and his followers prefer "purebloods" to "Mudbloods," some wizards discriminate against giants, others believe Muggles to be inferior, etc. If these are magical expressions of cultural prejudices, what do you make of the decision to represent such tensions through this metaphor? Is it too evasive or more effective?

4. Do the novels critique or sustain a class system? Are "wizards," as Pico Iyer suggests, "only regular Muggles who've been to the right school"? Because Hogwarts is available only to those privileged enough to be wizards, is it an elitist school? Or, because Malfoy's snobby attitude is not presented sympathetically, are the books really anti-elitist?

5. To a reader intrigued by Snape, Rowling advises, "Keep an eye on him" (Barnes and Noble Chat). So, who is Snape working for, really? Is he on Dumbledore's side? Voldemort's? Is he only looking out for himself? Put another way, is Snape's behavior motivated by a schoolboy grudge or by al-

legiance to Voldemort? Is Snape petty or evil? What will his role be in the final three novels?

6. Consider the character of Wormtail (a.k.a. Peter Pettigrew). What motivates him? When Harry is upset that he saved Pettigrew's life, Dumbledore says, "Pettigrew owes his life to you. You have sent Voldemort a deputy who is in your debt. When one wizard saves another wizard's life, it creates a certain bond between them . . . and I'm much mistaken if Voldemort wants his servant in the debt of Harry Potter." When Harry says he doesn't want a bond with Pettigrew, Dumbledore replies, "The time may come when you will be very glad you saved Pettigrew's life" (*Prisoner of Azkaban* 311). Does Pettigrew telling Voldemort that his return to power could be accomplished without Harry Potter (*Goblet of Fire* 13–14) seem motivated by a desire to help Harry or by Pettigrew's cowardice? What will his role be in the remaining novels? Will Pettigrew remain Voldemort's faithful servant? Will he help Harry? Are these questions complicated further by Sirius Black's suggestion in chapter 19 of *Prisoner of Azkaban* that other Death Eaters might turn against Pettigrew?

7. In *Goblet of Fire*, Ron remarks, "Percy loves rules," and he wonders whether his brother would send a family member to Azkaban if it would advance his career (463). Reflect on the role of bureaucracy in the novels. Does his tendency to side with bureaucracy make Percy susceptible to the same sorts of errors made by Cornelius Fudge and Mr. Crouch, errors that ultimately (if unintentionally) help Lord Voldemort? Might we expect him—albeit unwittingly—to aid Voldemort by following the letter of the law instead of its spirit? Will he side with Crouch or with his family?

8. Think about the individual's relationship to the law—Hogwarts's rules, national wizarding laws, international wizarding laws—and then think about those who operate outside of these laws. Focus in particular on the characters of Sirius Black, Barty Crouch, Ludo Bagman, Arthur Weasley, the Weasley twins, Harry, Ron, and Hermione, all of whom either bend the rules or break the law. Which rules or laws do they break? Does Rowling see their behavior as justified? Why, or why not? How does she gauge whether a law or a rule is just or unjust? When are laws or rules susceptible to challenge?

9. When asked why her central character is male, Rowling replied that, having imagined Harry as the hero, she could not easily change him into

Harriet Potter. She has also said, "Hermione is such a good friend [. . .] that I don't feel I have short-changed girls!" ("J. K. Rowling chat transcript"). However, Donna Harrington-Lueker faults the books' for "subtle sexism," maintaining that "none of the girls or women in *Goblet of Fire* escapes shrillness, giddiness or fear." Hermione is "bossy, shrill, exasperating and meddlesome," "the stereotypical good girl who completes her work ahead of time, chides her friends for breaking rules and always has her hand up in class." Christine Schoefer writes, "Girls, when they are not downright silly or unlikable, are helpers, enablers and instruments." Of the professors, Minerva McGonagall is "stern," overly "bound by" rules, and too emotional in a crisis; Sybill Trelawney is "a misty, dreamy, dewy charlatan." Do you agree with these analyses? Do the *Harry Potter* novels uphold stereotypical gender roles? Why, or why not? What would the books be like if Hermione was the central character instead of Harry?

10. Why has Rowling drawn connections between Voldemort and Harry? In linking these characters so closely, is she suggesting some kinship between opposites? Are good and evil bound closely together? Can you think of other characters in the series who, though they appear to be opposites, are in fact more alike than we initially suspect?

11. Nigel Newton, the chief executive of Bloomsbury Publishing, has predicted that the *Harry Potter* books "will still be bought for children in 100 years' time" (Prynn). Is he merely promoting his company's interests? Will the Potter novels be classics? What do they share in common with other classics? In your answer, decide how you'll define the word "classic." Does it denote "classic literature for children," "classic fantasy," "classic British literature"? Something else? In defining the term, choose some points of comparison. If you think they are classics, are we to compare the novels with works by Lewis Carroll? C. S. Lewis? Charles Dickens? If not, what would be your point of comparison? Enid Blyton? Against what other works are we to measure the *Harry Potter* series? What are the criteria of a classic?

12. Look for clues. As illustrated by Sirius Black's motorbike (mentioned in the first chapter of the first book), Rowling often leaves hints in her novels, looking ahead to future plot developments. Identify those hints she's already developed, and see if you can spot ones that will be addressed in future novels.

Notes

1. The "K" did not appear on her birth certificate, leading some to speculate that she did not adopt "Kathleen"—her grandmother's name—as her middle name until later in life (Savill).

2. At the very least, Rowling joins other artists who either lived or worked in the area: J. M. W. Turner painted Chepstow Castle here, and Dennis Potter, author of *The Singing Detective* (TV miniseries,1986) and *Pennies from Heaven* (miniseries, 1978; film,1981), grew up near the Forest of Dean, too.

3. This appears to be not a direct quotation but a paraphrase of the sentiments expressed in Woolf's essay on Austen, first published in *The Common Reader* (1925) and included in volume 1 of Woolf's *Collected Essays* (1966). In the essay, Woolf writes, "Jane Austen is thus a mistress of much deeper emotion than appears on the surface. She stimulates us to supply what is not there. What she offers is, apparently, a trifle, yet is composed of something that expands in the reader's mind and endows with the most enduring form of life scenes which are outwardly trivial" (148). Recalling a scene from Austen's *Mansfield Park*, Woolf says, "The discrimination is so perfect, the satire so just, that, consistent though it is, almost escapes our notice. [. . .] That elusive quality is, indeed, often made up of very different parts, which it needs a peculiar genius to bring together" (150).

4. In volume 3, chapter 27 of *Pride and Prejudice*, after Darcy proposed (for the second time) but before Elizabeth has told her family, Austen writes,

"Elizabeth, agitated and confused, rather *knew* that she was happy, than *felt* herself to be so" (331).

5. Carroll's riddle about the raven and the writing-desk, which appears in the "Mad Tea-Party" chapter of *Alice in Wonderland*, has many solutions, but Carroll's favorite was "Because it can produce a few notes, tho they are *very* flat; and it is nevar put with the wrong end in front"—the word "nevar" being "raven" backwards (72). Martin Gardner has collected many other solutions in *The Annotated Alice: The Definitive Edition* (71–73). Readers of *Harry Potter and the Chamber of Secrets* will know that "TOM MARVOLO RIDDLE." spells out "I AM LORD VOLDEMONT."

6. If the gryphon in chapters 9, 10, and all of *Alice in Wonderland* did not make an impression on Rowling, perhaps the fact that gryphon is the emblem to Oxford's Trinity College (as well as the symbol of the city of London) did influence the school crest of Hogwarts, which includes a gryffin for Gryffindor house. Similarly, Rowling's Sir Cadogan, who has a tendency to tumble from his steed, recalls Carroll's White Knight, and both characters share Cervantes's Don Quixote as a literary ancestor.

7. I am indebted to Gloria Hardman for alerting me to Rowling's use of primes in this chapter. For more on Carroll's games, numerical and otherwise, see Martin Gardner's *The Universe in a Handkerchief: Lewis Carroll's Mathematical Recreations, Games, Puzzles, and Word Plays* (1996).

8. The Bloomsbury editions total 1,427 pages; the Scholastic editions total 1,819 pages.

9. Daniel Johnson's reply to Hensher, published in the *Daily Telegraph* on January 29, offered the following rebuttal: "If *Harry Potter* outsells everything, this does not mean that adult culture is being infantilized, but that 'adult' novels lack imaginative power. What makes *Beowulf* compelling is also what gives *Harry Potter* its universal appeal."

10. Many cartoonists offered variations on these themes, such as Scott Willis of the *San Jose Mercury News*, who drew two parents watching *Survivor* while their son, a *Harry Potter* book in hand, asks, "COULD YOU TURN THAT DOWN? I'M TRYING TO READ" (July 12, 2000); and the *Los Angeles Times*'s Michael Ramirez, whose "Survivors" displayed a father and daughter reading *Harry Potter* together, having thrown out the television set, which sits in a garbage can full of articles about "reality TV" (July

14, 2000). In the electoral category, Fox News's Chris Hiers illustrated Al Gore with a lightning bolt on his head and round, Potter-esque glasses while Tipper Gore asks, "Oh *Al!* When you said you were going to start wearing glasses so you would look like *Harry*—I thought you meant *Truman* not *Potter!*"

Works Cited

Books by Rowling

Rowling, J. K. *Harry Potter and the Chamber of Secrets*. London: Blooms-
bury, 1998.
———. *Harry Potter and the Goblet of Fire*. London: Bloomsbury, 2000.
———. *Harry Potter and the Philosopher's Stone*. London: Bloomsbury, 1997.
———. *Harry Potter and the Prisoner of Azkaban*. London: Bloomsbury, 1999.
Scamander, Newt [J. K. Rowling]. *Fantastic Beasts and Where to Find Them*.
London: Bloomsbury and Obscurus Books, 2001.
Whisp, Kennilworthy [J. K. Rowling]. *Quidditch Through the Ages*. London:
Bloomsbury and WhizzHard Books, 2001.

Essays by Rowling

Rowling, J. K. Foreword. *Families Just Like Us: The One Parent Families
Good Book Guide*. London: Young Book Trust and National Council for
One Parent Families, 2000.
———. "Let me tell you a story." *Sunday Times* (London) 21 May 2000.
———. "JK Rowling's diary." *Sunday Times* (London) 26 July 1998.
———. "The not especially fascinating life so far of J. K. Rowling." 1998
(http://www.okukbooks.com/harry/rowling.htm)

Profiles and Interviews

Adler, Margot. Profile of J. K. Rowling. *All Things Considered*. National Public Radio. 3 Dec. 1998.

Barnes and Noble Chat with J. K. Rowling. 20 Oct. 2000. (http://www.hpnetwork.f2s.com/jkrowling/jkrbnchat.html).

Carey, Joanna. "Who hasn't met Harry?" *The Guardian* 16 Feb. 1999 (http://www.guardianunlimited.co.uk/Archive/Article/0,4273,3822242,00.html [16 Aug. 1999.])

Cochrane, Lynne. "Harry's Home." *Sunday Times* (London) 2 July 2000.

Fraser, Lindsey. *Telling Tales: An Interview with J. K. Rowling*. London: Mammoth, 2000.

Gray, Paul. "Wild about Harry." *Time* 20 Sept. 1999.

Hattenstone, Simon. "Harry, Jessie, and Me." *The Guardian Weekend* 8 July 2000: 32+.

Jerome, Helen M. "Welcome back, Potter." *Book* May–June 2000: 40–45.

"JK Rowling chat: 4 May 2000." (http://www.geocites.com/harrypotterfans/jkraolchat.html).

"J.K. Rowling chat transcript." c. Oct. 2000 (http://www.hpnetwork.f2s.com/jkraolchat.html [7 Nov. 2000]).

"J. K. Rowling reads for the magic." *O Magazine* Jan. 2001: 150–51.

"J. K. Rowling's bookshelf." *O Magazine* Jan. 2001: 155.

Johnstone, Anne. "Happy ending, and that's for beginners." *The Herald* (Glasgow) 24 June 1997: 15+.

———. "A kind of magic." *The Herald Saturday Magazine* 8 July 2000: 8–12.

"Magic, mystery, and mayhem: an interview with J. K. Rowling." (http://www.amazon.com/exec/obidos/ts/feature/6230/ [16 Dec. 1999]).

Mehren, Elizabeth. "Upward and onward toward book seven—her way." *Los Angeles Times* 25 Oct. 2000: E1+.

National Press Club. Reading and question-and-answer session. 20 Oct. 1999. *Book-TV* C-SPAN2 6 Nov. 1999.

Phillips, Mark. "Pure magic." *CBS Sunday Morning* 26 Sept. 1999.

Rosie O'Donnell Show. ABC. 21 June 1999.

Solomon, Evan. "J. K. Rowling interview." *Hot Type*. CBC July 2000 [(http://cbc.ca/programs/sites/hottype_rowlingcomplete.html)]).

Stahl, Lesley. Profile of J. K. Rowling. *60 Minutes*. CBS 12 Sept. 1999.

"Transcript of J. K. Rowling's live interview on Scholastic.com." 3 Feb. 2000 (http://www.scholastic.com/harrypotter/author/transcript1.htm).

Treneman, Ann. "Harry and me." *The Times* (London) 30 June 2000.

"Transcript of J. K. Rowling's live interview on Scholastic.com." 16 Oct. 2000 (http://www.scholastic.com/harrypotter/author/transcript2.htm).

Weeks, Linton. "Charmed, I'm sure; the enchanting success story of Harry Potter's creator, J. K. Rowling." *Washington Post* 20 Oct. 1999: C1.

Weir, Margaret. "Of magic and single motherhood." *Salon* 31 March 1999 (http://www.salon.com/mwt/feature/1999/03/cov_31featureb.html).

Other Works that Mention Rowling or *Potter*

"The American way of giving." *The Economist* 25 Jan. 2001.

Barnes, Julian E. "Dragons and flying brooms: Mattel shows off its line of Harry Potter toys." *New York Times* 1 March 2000: C1. (http://www.nytimes.com/2001/03/01/business/01ADCO.html?pagewanted=all&0301ins ide).

Bethune, Brian. "The Rowling connection: how a young Toronto girl's story touched an author's heart." *Maclean's* 6 Nov. 2000: 92.

Bloomsbury Publishing Plc: Annual Report and Accounts 1998.

Bloomsbury Publishing Plc: Annual Report and Accounts 1999.

Cowell, Alan. "Investors and children alike give rave reviews to Harry Potter books." *New York Times* 18 Oct. 1999 (http://www.nytimes.com/library/books/101899harry-potter.html).

Demetriou, Danielle. "Harry Potter and the source of inspiration." *Daily Telegraph* (London) 1 July 2000: 3.

Egan, Kelly. "Potter author thrills 15,000: J. K. Rowling leads 'revolution'." *The Ottowa Citizen* 25 Oct. 2000: A3.

Gibbons, Fiachra. "Harry Potter banned from paper's bestseller list." *Guardian Home Pages* 17 July 1999: 6.

Glaister, Dan. "Debut author and single mother sells children's book for £100,000." *The Guardian* 8 July 1997: 4.

Holt, Karen Jenkins. "Spreading the Potter Magic." *Brill's Content* April 2001: 98.

Johnson, Sarah. "Just wild about Harry." *The Times* (London) 23 Apr. 1999.

Judge, Elizabeth. "Rowling rejects Tory's family 'norm'." *The Times* (London) 6 Dec. 2000.

Levine, Arthur A., with Doreen Carvajal. "Why I paid so much." *New York Times* 13 Oct. 1999: C14.

Loer, Stephanie. "'Harry Potter' is taking publishing world by storm." *Boston Globe* 3 Jan. 1999: M10.

Macdonald, Hugh. "Potter's deal. . . or the importance of being Harry." *The Herald Saturday Magazine* 8 July 2000: 8–12.

Mutter, John, and Jim Milliot. "Harry Potter and the weekend of fiery sales." *Publishers Weekly* 17 July 2000: 76.

"Now it's Doctor Rowling." *Post and Courier* (Charleston, South Carolina). 15 July 2000: 2-A.

Prynn, Jonathan. "Potter to join Pooh and classics." *The Evening Standard* 6 Oct. 1999: 23.

"A Rowling Timeline." *Book* May-June 2000: 40–45.

Rustin, Susanna. "They're all just wild about Harry." *Financial Times* (London) 22 Apr. 2000: 9.

Savill, Richard. "Harry Potter and the mystery of J K's lost initial." *The Daily Telegraph* (London) 19 July 2000: 3.

Sayid, Ruki. "The Million-Hers; 50 Top Earning Women in the British Isles." *The Mirror* 18 Oct. 1999: 11.

"Scholastic joins J.K. Rowling to publish two Harry Potter–inspired books for charity." Press Release. 20 Nov. 2000 (http://www.scholastic.com/aboutscholastic/news/press00/press_11.20.00.htm).

"Turning a page at the Book Review." *INSIDE The New York Times* Fall 2000: 1–3.

Trueland, Jennifer. "Author's ex-husband gets in on the Harry Potter act." *The Scotsman* 15 Nov. 1999: 3.

"U.K.'s number one best-seller, 'Harry Potter and the Sorcerer's Stone,' tops best-seller charts in U.S." *Business Wire* 7 Dec. 1998.

Walker, Andrew. "Edinburgh author is elated as America goes potty over Potter." *The Scotsman* 29 Oct. 1998: 7.

Reviews and Editorials

Acocella, Joan. "Under the spell." *New Yorker* 31 July 2000: 74–78.

Blacker, Terence. "Why does everyone like Harry Potter?" *The Independent* (London) 13 July 1999: 4.

Bloom, Harold. "Can 35 million book buyers be wrong? Yes." *Wall Street Journal* 11 July 2000: A26.

Blume, Judy. "Is Harry Potter evil?" *New York Times* 22 Oct. 1999: A27. Repr. in *National Coalition Against Censorship* 76 (Winter 1999–2000) (http://www.ncac.org/cen_news/cn76harrypotter.html).

Bradman, Tony. "Mayhem wherever he flits." *Daily Telegraph* (London) 10 Oct. 1998.

Briggs, Julia. "Fighting the forces of evil." *Times Literary Supplement* 22 Dec. 2000.

Bruce, Ian S. "Wizard read lives up to hype." *Sunday Herald* 9 July 2000: 3.

Cohen, Whitaker E. "Hands off Harry!" Letter to the editor. *New Yorker* 18 & 25 Oct. 1999: 16.

Craig, Amanda. "Harry Potter and the Prisoner of Azkaban." *New Statesman* 12 July 1999: 74.

Crittenden, Daniele. "Boy meets book." *Wall Street Journal* 26 Nov. 1999: W13.

Dirda, Michael. "Harry Potter and the Chamber of Secrets." *Washington Post* 4 July 1999.

Donahue, Deirdre. "'Goblet of Fire' burns out." *USA Today* 10 July 2000: 1D.

Dubail, Jean. "Finding children's magic in world of Harry Potter. "*The Plain Dealer* (Cleveland) 13 June 1999: 10-I.

Dunbar, Robert. "Simply wizard." *The Irish Times* 17 July 1999.

Fraser, Lindsey. "Volumes of choice for the holidays." *The Scotsman* 28 June 1997: 15.

Galloway, Jim. "Harry Potter: school lets hero off hook." *Atlanta Journal and Constitution* 13 Oct. 1999: 1B.

Gilson, Nancy. "Sorcerer's Stone looks like a real page-turner. *Columbus Dispatch* 17 Sept. 1998: Weekender, p. 20.

Gleick, Peter H. "Harry Potter, minus a certain flavour." *New York Times* 10 July 2000: A25.

Hainer, Cathy. "Second time's still a charm." *USA Today* 27 May 1999: 1D.

———. "Third time's another charmer for 'Harry Potter' " *USA Today* 8 Sept. 1999: 1D.

Hall, Dinah. "Children's books: junior fiction." *Sunday Telegraph* 27 July 1997: 14.

————. "Children's books for summer: fiction." *Sunday Telegraph* 19 July 1998: Books, p. 12.

Harrington-Lueker, Donna. "'Harry Potter' lacks for true heroines." *USA Today* 11 July 2000: 17A.

Hensher, Philip. "Harry Potter, give me a break." *The Independent* (London) 25 January 2000: 1.

Hopkinson, Victoria. "Walks on the wild side and on the mild side." *Financial Times* (London) 4 Oct. 1997: 6.

Iyer, Pico. "The playing fields of Hogwarts." *New York Times Book Review* 10 Oct. 1999: 39.

Johnson, Sarah. "First review: new Harry Potter 'a cracker'." *The Times* (London) 8 July 2000: 1–2.

————. "Go for good writing." *The Times* (London) 23 Aug. 1997.

Johnstone, Anne. "Fun is brought to book." *The Herald* (Glasgow) 4 July 1998: 14.

Johnson, Daniel. "The monster of children's books JK Rowling shows originality and imagination: why then has she inspired such vitriol?" *Daily Telegraph* 29 Jan. 2000: 24.

Judah, Hettie. "Harry is pure magic." *The Herald* (Glasgow) 15 July 1999: 20.

King, Stephen. "Wild about Harry." *New York Times Book Review* 23 July 2000: 13–14.

Kipen, David. " J. K. Rowling's fantasy series hits an awkward teenage phase with 'Goblet'." *San Francisco Chronicle* 10 July 2000.

Levi, Jonathan. "Pottermania." *Los Angeles Times* 16 July 2000: Book Review, p. 1.

Lively, Penelope. "Harry's in robust form, although I'm left bug-eyed." *The Independent* (London) 13 July 2000: 5.

Lockerbie, Catherine. "Just wild about Harry." *The Scotsman* 9 July 1998: 12.

————. "Magical mystery tour de force." *The Scotsman* 10 July 1999: 11.

Macguire, Gregory. "Lord of the golden snitch." *New York Times Book Review* 5 Sept. 1999: 12.

Macmonagle, Niall. "The season of the wizard." *The Irish Times* 15 July 2000: 69.

Maslin, Janet. "At last, the wizard gets back to school." *New York Times* 10 July 2000: E1.

McCrum, Robert. "Plot, plot, plot that's worth the weight." *The Observer* 9 July 2000.

Parravano, Martha P. "J.K. Rowling, *Harry Potter and the Chamber of Secrets.*" *Horn Book* July–August 1999: 74.

Phelan, Laurence. "Books: Christmas dystopia; parents, ghosts, the future, bullying and lemonade." *The Independent* (London) 6 Dec. 1998: 12.

Power, Carla, with Shehnaz Suterwalla. "A literary sorceress." *Newsweek* 7 Dec. 1998: 7.

Radosh, Daniel. "Why American kids don't consider Harry Potter an insufferable prig." *New Yorker* 20 Sept. 1999: 54, 56.

Rosenberg, Liz. "A foundling boy and his corps of wizards." *Boston Globe* 1 Nov. 1998: L2.

———. Harry Potter's back again." *Boston Globe* 18 July 1999: K3.

———. "Making much of memories." *Boston Globe* 19 Sept. 1999: H2.

Safire, William. "Besotted with Potter." *New York Times* 27 Jan. 2000: A27.

Sawyer, Kem Knapp. "Orphan Harry and his Hogwarts mates work their magic stateside." *St. Louis Post-Dispatch* 13 June 1999: F12.

Schoefer, Christine. "Harry Potter's girl trouble." *Slate* 13 Jan. 2000 (http://www.salon.com/books/feature/2000/01/13/potter/index.html?CP =SAL&DN=650).

Sutton, Roger. "Potter's Field." *Horn Book* Sept.–Oct. 1999: 500–501.

Taylor, Alan. "We all know about the hype but is J K Rowling really up with the greats?" *Scotland on Sunday* 11 July 1999: 15.

Will, George F. "Harry Potter: a wizard's return." *Washington Post* 4 July 2000: A19.

Wynne-Jones, Tim. "Harry Potter and the blaze of publicity: on the whole, the junior wizard deserves it all." *The Ottawa Citizen* 16 July 2000: C16.

Winerip, Michael. "Children's books." *New York Times Book Review* 14 Feb. 1999 (http://www.nytimes.com/books/99/02/14/reviews/990214.14childrt .html).

Zipp, Yvonne. "Harry Potter swoops into great adventures." *Christian Science Monitor* 14 Jan. 1999: 19.

———. "Swooping to stardom." *Christian Science Monitor* 17 June 1999: 19.

Literary Criticism and Essay-Reviews

Gish, Kimbra Wilder. "Hunting down Harry Potter: an exploration of religious concerns about children's literature." *Horn Book* May–June 2000: 263–271.

Grynbaum, Gail A. "The secrets of Harry Potter." *San Francisco Jung Institute Library Journal* 19.4 (2001): 17–48.

Kantor, Jodi, and Judith Shulevitz. "The new Harry: Riotous, rushed, and remarkable." *Slate* 10–13 July 2000 (http://slate.msn.com/code/Book-Club/BookClub.asp?Show=7/10/00&idMessage=5648&idBio=183).

Lurie, Alison. "Not for Muggles." *New York Review of Books* 16 Dec. 1999 (http://www.nybooks.com/nyrev/WWWfeatdisplay.cgi?19991216006).

Scott, A. O., and Polly Shulman. "Is Harry Potter the new *Star Wars*?" *Slate* 23–26 Aug. 1999 (http://www.slate.com/code/BookClub/BookClub.asp?Show=8/23/99&idMessage=3472&idBio=111).

Tucker, Nicholas. "The rise and rise of Harry Potter." *Children's Literature in Education* 30.4 (Dec. 1999): 221–234.

Zipes, Jack. "The virtue (and vice) of stolid sameness: Harry sells millions, not because he's new, but because he's as old as King Arthur." *The Ottawa Citizen* 4 Feb. 2001: C15. Repr. from Zipes' *Sticks and Stones: The Troublesome Success of Children's Literature from Slovenly Peter to Harry Potter.*

Teacher's Guides

Beech, Linda Ward. *Scholastic Literature Guide: Harry Potter and the Chamber of Secrets by J. K. Rowling.* New York: Scholastic, 2000.

——. *Scholastic Literature Guide: Harry Potter and the Goblet of Fire by J. K. Rowling.* New York: Scholastic, 2000.

——. *Scholastic Literature Guide: Harry Potter and the Prisoner of Azkaban by J. K. Rowling.* New York: Scholastic, 2000.

——. *Scholastic Literature Guide: Harry Potter and the Sorcerer's Stone by J. K. Rowling.* New York: Scholastic, 2000.

Schafer, Elizabeth D. *Beacham's Sourcebooks for Teaching Young Adult Fiction: Exploring Harry Potter.* Osprey, FL: Beacham Publishing Corp., 2000.

Rowling Mentioned in Other Contexts

Aaronovitch, David. "Harry Potter and the menace of global capitalism." *The Independent* 28 Sept. 2000. (http://www.independent.co.uk/enjoyment/Books/Reviews/200009/thursbook280900.shtml).

Collins, Gail. "An ode to July." *New York Times* 11 July 2000: A31.

——. "Rudy's Identity Crisis." *New York Times* 14 April 2000.

Dowd, Maureen. "Dare speak his name." *New York Times* 22 Oct. 2000: 15.

Friedman, Thomas L. "Lebanon and the Goblet of Fire." *New York Times* 11 July 2000: 31.

Rose, Matthew, and Emily Nelson. "Potter cognoscenti all know a Muggle when they see one." *Wall Street Journal* 18 Oct. 2000: A1, A10.

"What if Quidditch, the enchanted sport of wizards and witches featured in the Harry Potter books, were regulated by the NCAA?" *Sports Illustrated* 21 Aug. 2000: 33.

Williams, Geoff. "Harry Potter and . . . the trials of growing a business . . . the rewards of independence and ownership." *Entrepreneur* Feb. 2001: 62–65.

Cartoons and Humor

Anderson, Nick. "Reality T.V." *Louisville Courier-Journal* 9 July 2000 (Repr. http://cagle.slate.msn.com/news/harrypotter/harry4.asp).

Browne, Bob. "Hi and Lois." 19 March 2001.

Conley, Darby. "Get Fuzzy." 22 June 2001.

"*Harry Potter* books spark rise in satanism among children." *The Onion* July 2000 (http://www.theonion.com/onion3625/harry_potter.html).

Johnston, Lynn. "For Better or For Worse." 1 Aug. 2000.

——. "For Better or For Worse." 21 Jan. 2001.

Keane, Bil. "Family Circus." 9 Apr. 2000.

Keane, Jeff and Bil. "Family Circus." 29 Oct. 2000.

——. "Family Circus." 31 Oct. 2000.

——. "Family Circus." 31 Dec. 2000.

Ohman, Jack. "Gore-Potter 2000." Repr. *Washington Post National Weekly Edition* 24 July 2000: 27.

Ramirez, Michael. "Survivors." *Los Angeles Times* 14 July 2000. (Repr. http://cagle.slate.msn.com/news/harrypotter/main.asp).

Ramsey, Marshall. "Old technology-1. New technology-0." *Clarion Ledger* (Jackson, Mississippi). 8 July 2000 (Repr. http://cagle.slate.msn.com/ news/harrypotter/harry3.asp).

Schulz, Charles. "Peanuts." 8 Nov. 1999.

Wasserman, Dan. "I can already see how it ends—the dark forces win." *Washington Post National Weekly Edition* 24 July 2000:28.

Willis, Scott. "COULD YOU TURN THAT DOWN? I'M TRYING TO READ!" *San Jose Mercury News* 12 July 2000. (Repr.http://cagle .slate.msn.com/news/harrypotter/harry9.asp).

Young, Dean, and Denis Lebrun. "Blondie." 4 Dec. 2000.

Other Works Cited

Adams, Richard. *Watership Down*. 1972. New York: Avon Books, 1975.

Anstey, F. *Vice Versa, or, A Lesson to Fathers:* 1882. London: Smith, Elder, & Co., 1911.

Austen, Jane. *Emma.* 1815. Oxford and New York: Oxford UP, 1992.

———. *Mansfield Park.* 1814. New York: Penguin, 1966.

———. *Northanger Abbey.* 1818. New York: Penguin, 1972.

———. *Pride and Prejudice.* 1813. Oxford and New York: Oxford UP, 1991.

Baum, L. Frank. *The Wizard of Oz.* 1900. New York: Oxford, 1997.

Blyton, Enid. *Fire Get Into a Fix.* 1958. Revised 1991. London: Hodder Children's Books, 2000.

———. *Five on Finniston Farm.* 1960. Revised 1990. London: Hodder Children's Books, 2000.

Carroll, Lewis. *The Annotated Alice: Definitive Edition.* Introduction and Notes by Martin Gardner. Illustrations by John Tenniel. New York: W.W. Norton & Co., 2000.

Clueless. Dir. Amy Heckerling, Perf. Alicia Silverstone, Stacey Dash, Paul Rudd. Paramount Pictures, 1995.

Cott, Jonathan. *Pipers at the Gates of Dawn: The Wisdom of Children's Literature.* New York: Random House, 1983.

Dahl, Roald. *Charlie and the Chocolate Factory.* 1964. Revised 1973. New York: Alfred A. Knopf, 1973.

———. *James and the Giant Peach.* 1961. New York: Puffin Books, 1988.

Doyle, Roddy. *The Woman Who Walked Into Doors:* New York: Penguin, 1996.

Gallico, Paul. *Manxmouse*. London: Heinemann, 1968.

Gardner, Martin. *The Universe in a Handkerchief: Lewis Carroll's Mathematical Recreations, Games, Puzzles, and Word Plays*. New York: Copernicus, 1996.

Ibbotson, Eva. *The Secret of Platform 13*. 1994. New York: Puffin, 1999.

Jones, Diana Wynne. *Charmed Life*. 1997. New York: Beech Tree, 1998.

———. *The Lives of Christopher Chant*. 1988. New York: Beech Tree (William Morrow), 1998.

———. *The Magicians of Caprona*. 1980. New York: Beech Tree, 1999.

———. *Witch Week*. 1982. New York: Beech Tree, 1997.

Kafka, Franz. "A Hunger Artist." 1924. *Selected Stories of Franz Kafka*. 1936. New York: Random House, 1952. 188–201.

LeGuin, Ursula K. *A Wizard of Earthsed*. 1968. New York: Bantam, 1975.

Lewis, C. S. *Letters to Children*. Ed. Lyle W. Dorsett and Marjorie Lamp Mead. New York: Macmillan Publishing Company, 1985.

———. *Of This and Other Worlds*. Ed. Walter Hooper. London: William Collins Sons & Co, 1982.

Mitford, Jessica. *Hons and Rebels*. London: V. Gollancz, 1960.

Nesbit, E. *The Five Children and It*. 1902. New York: Puffin, 1996.

———. *The Phoenix and the Carpet*. 1904. New York: Puffin, 1994.

———. *The Story of the Treasure Seekers*. 1899. New York: Puffin, 1994.

Orwell, George. "Boys' weeklies." 1940. *The Collected Essays, Journalism and Letters of George Orwell, Volume 1: An Age Like This, 1920–1940*. London: Secker & Warburg, 1968. 460–485.

Seuss, Dr. *Oh! The Places You'll Go!* New York: Random House, 1990.

Shakespeare, William. *The Winter's Tale*. 1610–11. *The Riverside Shakespeare*. Boston: Houghton Mifflin, 1974.

Strunk, William Jr., and E. B. White. *The Elements of Style*. Third Edition. New York: Macmillan Publishing, 1979.

Tolkien, J.R.R. *The Hobbit*. 1937. Revised edition 1982. New York: Ballantine Books, 1982.

White, E.B. *Charlotte's Web*. New York: Harper, 1952.

Woolf, Virginia. "Jane Austen." *Collected Essays*. Volume One. London: The Hogarth Press, 1966. 144–154.

Wordsworth, William. "Lines Composed a Few Miles Above Tintern Abbey." 1798. *Norton Anthology of English Literature*. Volume 2. Seventh Edition. New York: W.W. Norton & Co., 2000. 235–38.